New Groove
Fusion

Cross Cultural Fusion
Cooking That's Off The Hook

RICKY GANT

Copyright © 2023 Ricky Gant.

All rights reserved. No part of this book may be reproduced, stored, or transmitted by any means—whether auditory, graphic, mechanical, or electronic—without written permission of both publisher and author, except in the case of brief excerpts used in critical articles and reviews. Unauthorized reproduction of any part of this work is illegal and is punishable by law.

ISBN: 979-8-88640-328-2 (sc)
ISBN: 979-8-88640-329-9 (hc)
ISBN: 979-8-88640-330-5 (e)

Because of the dynamic nature of the Internet, any web addresses or links contained in this book may have changed since publication and may no longer be valid. The views expressed in this work are solely those of the author and do not necessarily reflect the views of the publisher, and the publisher hereby disclaims any responsibility for them.

One Galleria Blvd., Suite 1900, Metairie, LA 70001
(504) 702-6708

New Groove FUSION is dedicated to the memory of Ardessa Reeves, my Grandmom and Fleming Gant, my Dad. Will always be a part of who I am today, tomorrow and the future. Thank you for the wonderful memories, especially the ones that came right out of the kitchen.

ACKNOWLEDGEMENT

I would like to say thanks to my family my mom Joyce, Shawn my sister and my brother Kevin for encouragement love and support.

—Ricky Gant

To Chef Earl Arrowood for your dedication, guidance, inspiration, knowledge and wisdom.

—Ricky Gant

FOREWORD

Welcome to my celebration of food a cross cultural ethnic taste of flavors. And influences that have been merged and blended into what. I call new groove fusion cuisine. Which is a blend of Mediterranean, Caribbean, Asian, American, African, French, Cajun-Creole. The recipes in this cookbook range from mild to wild. I hope that you will have fun making and tasting the recipes in this cookbook. Bon Appetit!

—Chef Ricky Gant

COOKING TEMPERATURES

FOR OVEN

SLOW OVEN 300°f

SLOW MODERATE OVEN 325°F

MODERATE OVEN 350°F

QUICK MODERATE 375°F

MODERATE HOT 400°F

HOT OVEN 425°F TO 450°F

VERY HOT 475°F TO 500°F

FRYING TEMPERATUES

FOR DEEP-FRYING

350°F TO 375°F (175°C TO 190°C)

FOR SAUTE

FIRST PRE HEAT THE PAN BEFORE ADDING THE FOOD TO BE SAUTÉED AND THE FOOD MUST START COOKING AT HIGH HEAT OR THE FOOD WILL BEGIN T SIMMER ITS OWN JUICES. AND MEAT TO BE SAUTÉED ARE OFTEN DUSTED WITH FLOUR TO PREVENT STICKING.

FOR BROIL

BROILING IS A RAPID HIGH HEAT COOKING THAT IS USUALLY USED IN ONLY FOR TENDER CUTS OF MEATS, CHICKEN, FISH, SEAFOOD AND FEW VEGETABLE ITEMS.

TO BROIL TURN THE HEAT ON FULL AND THE COOKING TEMPERATURE IS REGULATED BY MOVING THE RACK NEARER TO OR FARTHER FROM THE HEAT SOURCE.

FOR GRILL

GRILLING IS DONE ON A OPEN GRID OVER A HEAT SOURCE AND WHICH MAY BE A CHARCOAL GRILL, A ELECTRIC GRILL OR A GAS GRILL AND THE COOKING TEMPERATURE IS REGULATED BY MOVING THE ITEMS OT BE COOKED TO THE HOTTER OR COOLER PLACES ON THE GRILL.

ROAST AND BAKE

TO ROAST AND TO BAKE MEANS TO COOK FOODS BY SURROUNDING THEM WITH HOT DRY AIR USUALLY IN AN OVEN THE TERM ROASTING USUALLY APPLIES TO MEATS AND POULTRY.

THE TERM BAKING USUALLY APPLIES TO BREADS, PASTRIES, VEGETABLES AND FISH.

PRESSURE FRYING

PRESSURE FRYING MEANS DEEP-FRYING IN A SPECIAL COVERED FRYER THAT TRAPS STEAM GIVEN OFF BY THE FOODS BEING COOKED AND INCREASES THE PRESSURE INSIDE THE KETTLE.

BROIL

TO BROIL MEANS TO COOK WITH RADIANT HEAT FROM ABOVE.

SAUTE

TO SAUTE MEANS TO COOK QUICKLY IN A SMALL AMOUNT OF FAT. USING SWEET BUTTER OR SALTED BUTTER, OLIVE OIL, VEGETABLE OIL, SAFFLOWER OIL, CANOLA OIL, GRAPESEED OIL, CORN OIL, PEANUT OIL.

PAN-FRY

TO PAN-FRY MEANS TO COOK IN A MODERATE AMOUNT OF FAT IN A PAN OVER MODERATE HEAT.

USING VEGETABLE OIL, SAFFLOWER OIL, CANOLA OIL, GRAPESEED OIL, CORN OIL, PEANUT OIL, OLIVE OIL.

DEEP FRY

TO DEEP-FRY MEANS TO COOK A FOOD SUBMERGED IN HOT FAT. USING CANOLA OIL, VEGETABLE OIL, PEANUT OIL.

SOME USES FOR HERBS AND SPICES (STANDARD)

Allspice, ginger, five-spice
Cakes, cookies, pies, desserts, puddings, preserves, relishes, yellow vegetables, breads, red meats, pork, game, fish, seafood, poultry, and beverages.

Basil, parsley, thyme, tarragon, rosemary, and sage
Tomatoes, salads, barbecue sauces, tomato sauces, soups, stews, vegetables, pasta salads, potato salads, most meats, game, fish, seafood, poultry, breads and chowders.

Celery seed
Meatloaf, beef, lamb, pork, veal, and vegetables.

Chili powders
Vegetable and beef chili, cocktail and barbecue sauces, egg dishes, meat, poultry, veal, pork, fish, seafood, wild game and soups, stews, and chowders.

Garlic
Almost all types of red meats, poultry, fish, seafood, game, sauces, breads, soups and stews, salad dressings, marinades, dips, and nearly all vegetables.

Black pepper, white pepper, crushed red pepper
Almost all types of red meats, poultry, fish, seafood, game, soups, sauces, stews, chowders, pastas, rice, potatoes, all types of vegetables, marinades, and dips.

Salt
Nearly everything listed above.

WHEN THE RECIPE CALLS FOR...

9-inch pie plate
8 x 1¼-inch layer cake pan – C
7 ⅜ x 3 ⅝ x 2¼-inch loaf pan – A

6-cup baking dish
8 or 9 x 1½-inch layer cake pan – C
10-inch pie plate
8½ x 3 ⅝ x 2 ⅝-inch loaf pan – A

8-cup baking dish
8 x 8 x 2-inch square pan – D
11 x 7 x 1½-inch baking pan
9 x 5 x 3-inch loaf pan – A

10-cup baking dish
9 x 9 x 2-inch square pan
11¾ x 7½ x 1¾-inch baking pan – D
15 x 10 x 1-inch jellyroll pan

12-cup baking dish or over

12 1/3 x 8½ x 2-inch glass baking pan	12 cups
13 x 9 x 2-inch metal baking pan	15 cups
14 x 10 ½ x 2½-inch roasting pan	19 cups

TOTAL VOLUME OF VARIOUS SPECIAL BAKING PANS

Tube Pans

7½ x 3-inch "Bundt" tube – K	6 cups
9 x 3½-inch fancy tube or "Bundt" pan – J or K	9 cups
9 x 3½-inch angel cake pan – H	12 cups
10 x 3¾-inch "Bundt" or "Crownburst" pan – K	12 cups
9 x 3½-inch fancy tube – J	12 cups
10 x 4-inch fancy tube mold (kugelhupf) – J	16 cups
10 x 4-inch angel cake pan – H	18 cups

Springform Pans

8 x 3-inch pan – B	12 cups
9 x 3-inch pan – B	16 cups

Ring Mold

8½ x 2¼-inch mold – E	4½ cups
9¼ x 2¾-inch mold – E	8 cups

Charlotte Mold

6 x 4¼-inch mold – G	7½ cups

Brioche Pan

9½ x 3¼-inch pan – F	8 cups

QUANTITIES TO SERVE 100 PEOPLE

Coffee	3 lbs.
Cream	3 qts.
Whipping cream	4 pts.
Milk	6 gallons
Fruit cocktail	2½ gallons
Fruit juice	4 #10 cans
Tomato juice	4 #10 cans
Soup	5 gallons
Hot Dogs	25 lbs.
Meat loaf	18 to 22 lbs.
Ham	40 lbs.
Rolls	200
Butter	3 lbs.
Potato salad	3½ to 4 gals.
Fruit salad	20 qts.
Vegetable salad	20 qts.
Lettuce	16 lg. heads
Salad dressing	3 qts.
Jell-O	2½ qts.
Pies	18
Cakes	8
Ice cream	4 gallons
Beef	40 lbs.
Roast pork	40 lbs.
Hamburger	30 to 36 lbs.
Chicken for chicken pie	40 lbs.
Potatoes	35 lbs.
Scalloped potatoes	4 gals.
Spaghetti	5 gals.
Vegetables	4 #10 cans
Baked beans	5 gals.
Beets	25 lbs.
Cauliflower	18 lbs.
Cabbage for slaw	16 lbs.
Carrots	24 lbs.
Corn	2 #10 cans
Bread	10 loaves
Cheese	3 lbs.
Olives	1¾ lbs.
Pickles	2 qts.
Nuts	3 lbs.

To serve 50 people, divide by 2. To serve 25 people, divide by 4. Cooking for a crowd? The season of the year rules the food choices to a degree. Also variety in flavor, texture, color, and form. Plan best use of refrigerator space. Decide type of service: buffet, family style, or served plates with waitresses.

CONTENTS OF CANS

Of the different sizes of cans used by commercial canners, the most common are:

Size	Average Contents
8 ounces	1 cup
picnic	1¼ cups
No. 300	1¾ cups
No. 1 tall	2 cups
No. 303	2 cups
No. 2	2½ cups
No. 2½	3½ cups
No. 3	4 cups
No. 10	12 to 13 cups

Simplified Measures

Measure	Equivalent
1 tablespoon	3 teaspoons
2 tablespoons	1 ounce
1 jigger	1½ ounces
¼ cup	4 tablespoons
1/3 cup	5 tablespoons plus 1 teaspoon
½ cup	8 tablespoons
1 cup	16 tablespoons
1 pint	2 cups
1 quart	4 cups
1 gallon	4 quarts
1 liter	4 cups plus 3 tablespoons
1 ounce (dry)	2 tablespoons
1 pound	16 ounces
2.21 pounds	35.3 ounces

Equivalents for Common Cooking Ingredients:

1 lb	Apples	3 or 4 medium
1 lb	Bananas	3 or 4 medium
1 lb	Beans, dried	5 to 6 cups cooked
1 quart	Berries	3½ cups
1 slice	Bread	½ cup crumbs
¼ lb	Cheese, grated	1 cup
1 oz	Chocolate, 1 square	1 T. melted
½ pint	Cream	1 cup
1 cup	Cream, heavy	2 cups whipped
1 lb	Flour, all-purpose	4 cups sifted
1 envelope	Gelatin	1 T.
1 tsp	Herbs, dried	1 T. fresh
2-3 T. juice	Lemon	1½ tsp. grated rind
1 cup dry	Macaroni	2¼ cups cooked
1 lb	Meat, diced	2 cups
1 lb	Mushrooms	5-6 cups sliced
¼ lb	Nuts, shelled	1 cup chopped
1 medium	Onion	½ cup chopped
6-8 T. juice	Orange	1/3-1/2 cup pulp
3 medium	Potatoes	1¾ - 2 cups mashed
1 cup uncooked	Rice	3 cups cooked
½ lb	Spaghetti	3½ - 4 cups cooked
1 lb	Sugar, confectioner's	4½ cups unsifted
1 lb	Sugar, granulated	2 cups
1 lb	Tomatoes	3 or 4 medium
1 lb	Walnuts in shell	1¾ cups chopped

SUBSTITUTIONS

For bread crumbs: Use crushed corn or wheat flakes, or other dry cereal. Or use potato flakes.

For butter: Use 7/8 cup of solid shortening plus ½ teaspoon of salt.

For fresh milk: To substitute 1 cup of fresh milk, use ½ cup each of evaporated milk and water. For 1 cup of whole milk, prepare 1 liquid cup of nonfat dry milk and 2½ teaspoons butter or margarine.

For sugar: Use brown sugar, although it will result in a slight molasses flavor.

For superfine sugar: Process regular granulated sugar in your blender.

For red and green sweet pepper:
Use canned pimientos.

For vanilla extract: Use grated lemon or orange rind for flavoring, instead. Or try a little cinnamon or nutmeg.

For flour: Use 1 tablespoon cornstarch instead of 2 tablespoons of flour. Or try using instant potatoes or cornmeal.

For buttermilk: Use 1 tablespoon of lemon juice or vinegar and enough fresh milk to make 1 cup. Let it stand 5 minutes before using.

For catsup: Use a cup of tomato sauce added to 1¼ cups of brown sugar, 2 tablespoons of vinegar, ¼ teaspoon of cinnamon and a dash of ground cloves and allspice.

For unsweetened chocolate: Use 1 tablespoon of shortening plus 3 tablespoons of unsweetened chocolate to equal 1 square of unsweetened chocolate.

For corn syrup: Use ¼ cup of water or other type of liquid called for in the recipe, plus 1 cup of sugar.

For eggs: Add 3 or 4 extra tablespoons of liquid called for in the recipe. Or, when you're 1 egg shy for a recipe that calls for many, substitute 1 teaspoon of cornstarch.

For cake flour: Use 7/8 cup of all-purpose flour for each cup of cake flour called for in a recipe. **For fresh herbs and spices:** Use 1/3 the amount of dried herbs or spices. Dried herbs are more concentrated.

For honey: To substitute 1 cup of honey, use 1¼ cups of sugar and ¼ cup of water or other liquid called for in the recipe.

OTHER SUBSTITUTIONS

For:	You Can Use:
1 T. cornstarch	2 T. flour OR 1½ T. quick cooking tapioca
1 C. cake flour	1 C. less 2 T. all-purpose flour
1 C. all-purpose flour	1 C. plus 2 T. cake flour
1 C. melted shortening	1 C. salad oil (may not be substituted for solid shortening)
1 C. milk	½ C. evaporated milk and ½ C. water
1 C. heavy cream	⅔ C. milk and ⅓ C. butter
1 C. heavy cream, whipped	⅔ C. well-chilled evaporated milk, whipped
Sweetened condensed milk	No substitution
1 egg	2 T. dried whole egg and 2 T. water
1 tsp. baking powder	¼ tsp. baking soda and 1 tsp. cream of tartar OR ¼ tsp. baking soda and ½ C. sour milk, buttermilk, or molasses; reduce other liquid ½ C.
1 C. sugar	1 C. honey; reduce other liquid ¼ C.; reduce baking temperature 25°
1 C. miniature marshmallows	About 10 large marshmallows, cut up

1 medium onion (2½" dia)	2 T. instant minced onion OR 1 tsp. onion powder OR 2 tsp. onion salt; reduce salt 1 tsp.
1 garlic clove	1/8 tsp. garlic powder OR ¼ tsp. garlic salt reduce salt ⅛ tsp.
1 T. fresh herbs	1 tsp. dried herbs OR ¼ tsp. powdered herbs OR ½ tsp. herb salt; reduce salt ¼ tsp.

Deep-Fat Frying Temperatures
Without a Thermometer

A one-inch cube of white bread will turn golden brown:

Temperature	Time
345° to 355°	65 seconds
355° to 365°	60 seconds
365° to 375°	50 seconds
375° to 385°	40 seconds
385° to 395°	20 seconds

Oven Temperatures

Slow	300°
Slow moderate	325°
Moderate	350°
Quick moderate	375°
Moderately hot	400°
Hot	425°
Very Hot	475°

FUSION PANTRY STAPLES

Herbs and Spices

Chinese Five Spice Powder
A spice mixture containing ground czechwan peppercorns, ground cloves, ground fennel seed, ground star anise and ground cinnamon. Good for stir frying, marinades, dipping sauces, BBQ sauces. Can be used as a seasoning for meats, fish and seafood, soups, salads and baking.

Caribbean Spice Seasoning
A spice mixture containing, or having a variation of, ground red and black peppercorns, cumin, fennel seed, red chili powder, salt, coriander, nutmeg, ginger, allspice, onion powder, garlic powder, thyme and oregano.

Island Spice Seasoning
A spice mixture containing, or having a variation of all of the above plus, dry ground jalapeno, Scotch bonnet and serrano chili peppers and adobo. Good for marinades, dipping sauces, BBQ sauces. Can be used as a seasoning for meats, fish and seafood, soups and salads.

Asian Spice Seasoning
A spice mixture containing, or having a variation of, curry leaves, citrus zests, turmeric, cumin, coriander, cinnamon, allspice, ginger, star anise, cloves. Good for marinades, dipping sauces and BBQ sauces. Can be used as a seasoning for meats, fish and seafood, soups and salads.

Southwest/Mexican Spice Seasoning
A spice mixture containing, or having a variation of, ancho chili, guajillo chili, serrano chili, jalapeno chili, pink peppercorns, cinnamon, onion powder, cumin, thyme, oregano and salt. Good for marinades, dipping sauces and BBQ sauces. Can be used as a seasoning for meats, fish and seafood, soups and salads.

Southern/Cajun Spice Seasoning

A spice mixture containing, or having a variation of, ancho chili, cayenne, cumin, mustard seed, red chili powder, black pepper, paprika, garlic powder, onion powder, cinnamon, ginger, salt and coriander. Good for marinades, dipping sauces and BBQ sauces. Can be used as a seasoning for meats, fish and seafood, soups and salads.

Italian/Mediterranean Spice Seasoning

A spice mixture containing, or having a variation of, garlic, onion, fennel seed, basil, oregano, thyme, tarragon, rosemary, paprika, white pepper, celery seed, sugar and parsley. Good for marinades and sauces. Can be used as a seasoning for meats, fish and seafood, soups and salads.

Oils and Seasoned Oils

Sesame Oil and Toasted Sesame Oil

These oils are made from sesame seeds and toasted sesame seeds and come in an array of colors, ranging from light golden to a rich, dark golden or amber color. These oils are used to add flavor and seasoning. They are aromatic but, once heated, they exhibit nutty sesame fragrance. Use in Asian and Caribbean cooking.

Canola Oil

If you're trying to maintain a healthier lifestyle, this would be our personal recommendation, since Canola oil is lower in saturated fat and very high in Omega 3's and 6's fatty acids. Canola is light and goes well with healthy salads and almost any of our dishes. We like to blend herbs and spices with Canola because the taste is clean and straight forward and the flavors of the herbs/spices come through well.

Peanut Oil

This oil is used in both Asian and Caribbean cooking. Its color ranges from golden to golden brown and, depending on how the oil is pressed, it may have a high smoke point. We prefer to use cold pressed peanut oil for our fusion cooking since it doesn't possess an overpowering peanut flavor.

Olive Oil and Extra Virgin Olive Oils
One of the most widely used and popular cooking oils used today, olive oil has been a staple in Euro-Mediterranean cooking for centuries. This oil is fragrant and fruity and very flavor intensive. Olive oil's flavor and color vary from region to region, with climate and soil quality, as well as pressing conditions, playing a crucial part in the end product's characteristics. It ranges in color from light to rich golden, with varying tints of green, depending on pressing and refining methods. Extra virgin olive oil is most widely used because of its healthy, fruity flavor and versatility in cooking. For frying or sautéing, use a regular olive oil or a blend.

Chili Oils and Infused Oils
Chili oils are made with some of the finest blend of chiles. They may include, Ancho, Jalapeno, Chipolte, Poblano, Anahiem, Thai, Jamaica Hot, Scotch Bonnet, Habanero, African Bird, Guiglio and Serrano. All of these chili peppers have their own unique flavor and heat intensity level. They also are sold in a variety of ways from fresh to sun dried to smoked and pickled. They have fruity like flavors and overtones. Chiles are prevalent in almost every part of the world, and, in almost every culture as a staple or key ingredient and a flavoring.

They can also be combined with other flavorings and ingredients to give even more depths of flavor and tastes. Chili oils use a variety of oils as a base like canola oil, olive oil, sesame oil, peanut oil and safflour oil. Usings these oils give and extra depth as well as flavor to your dishes. For instance, if you wanted to excentuate only the flavor of the chili pepper combined with ginger root only, then use a good canola oil. Canola oil has a neutral taste which is perfect in this case.

Infused oils can be made using the oils listed above as well. Infusing other elements like common to exotic herbs and spices, nuts and other fragrant ingredients.

FUSION FOOD PANTRY STAPLES

Herbs and Spices

Chinese Five Spice Powder
A spice mixture containing ground Szechwan peppercorns, ground cloves, ground fennel seed, ground star anise and ground cinnamon. Good for stir frying marinades, dipping sauces, BBQ sauces. Can be used as a seasoning for meats, fish and seafood, soups, salads and baking.

Caribbean Spice Seasoning
A spice mixture containing, or having a variation of, ground red and black peppercorns, cumin, fennel seed, red chili powder, salt, coriander, nutmeg, ginger, allspice, onion powder, garlic powder, thyme and oregano.

Island Spice Seasoning
A spice mixture containing, or having a variation of all of the above plus, dry ground jalapeno, Scotch bonnet and Serrano chili peppers and adobo. Good for marinades, dipping sauces, BBQ sauces. Can be used as a seasoning for meats, fish and seafood, soups and salads.

Asian Spice Seasoning
A spice mixture containing, or having a variation of, curry leaves, citrus zests, turmeric, cumin, coriander, cinnamon, allspice, ginger, star anise, cloves. Good for marinades, dipping sauces and BBQ sauces. Can be used as a seasoning for meats, fish and seafood, soups and salads.

Southwest/Mexican Spice Seasoning
A spice mixture containing, or having a variation of, ancho chili, guajillo chili, Serrano chili, jalapeno chili, pink peppercorns, cinnamon, onion powder, cumin, thyme, oregano and salt. Good for marinades, dipping sauces and BBQ sauces. Can be used as a seasoning for meats, fish and seafood, soups and salads.

Southern/Cajun Spice Seasoning
A spice mixture containing, or having a variation of, ancho chili, cayenne, cumin, mustard seed, red chili powder, black pepper, paprika, garlic powder, onion powder, cinnamon, ginger, salt and coriander. Good for marinades, dipping sauces and BBQ sauces. Can be used as a seasoning for meats, fish and seafood, soups and salads.

Italian/Mediterranean Spice Seasoning
A spice mixture containing, or having a variation of, garlic, onion, fennel seed, basil, oregano, thyme, tarragon, rosemary, paprika, white pepper, celery seed, sugar and parsley. Good for marinades and sauces. Can be used as a seasoning for meats, fish and seafood, soups and salads.

Oils and Seasoned Oils

Sesame Oil and Toasted Sesame Oil
These oils are made from sesame seeds and toasted sesame seeds and come in an array of colors, ranging from light golden to a rich, dark golden or amber color. These oils are used to add flavor and seasoning. They are aromatic but, once heated, they exhibit nutty sesame fragrance. Use in Asian and Caribbean cooking.

Canola Oil
If you're trying to maintain a healthier lifestyle, this would be our personal recommendation, since Canola oil is lower in saturated fat and very high in Omega 3's and 6's fatty acids. Canola is light and goes well with healthy salads and almost any of our dishes. We like to blend herbs and spices with Canola because the taste is clean and straight forward and the flavors of the herbs/spices come through well.

Peanut Oil
This oil is used in both Asian and Caribbean cooking. Its color ranges from golden to golden brown and, depending on how the oil is

pressed, it may have a high smoke point. We prefer to use cold pressed peanut oil for our fusion cooking since it doesn't possess an overpowering peanut flavor.

Olive Oil and Extra Virgin Olive Oils

One of the most widely used and popular cooking oils used today, olive oil has been a staple in Euro-Mediterranean cooking for centuries. This oil is fragrant and fruity and very flavor intensive. Olive oil's flavor and color vary from region to region, with climate and soil quality, as well as pressing conditions, playing a crucial part in the end product's characteristics. It ranges in color from light to rich golden, with varying tints of green, depending on pressing and refining methods. Extra virgin olive oil is most widely used because of its healthy, fruity flavor and versatility in cooking. For frying or sautéing, use a regular olive oil or a blend.

Chili Oils and Infused Oils

Chili oils are made with some of the finest blend of chilies. They may include, Ancho, Jalapeno, Chipotle, Poblano, Anaheim, Thai, Jamaica Hot, Scotch Bonnet, Habanero, African Bird, Guiglio and Serrano. All of these chili peppers have their own unique flavor and heat intensity level. They also are sold in a variety of ways from fresh to sun dried to smoked and pickled. They have fruity like flavors and overtones. Chiles are prevalent in almost every part of the world, and, in almost every culture as a staple or key ingredient and a flavoring.

They can also be combined with other flavorings and ingredients to give even more depths of flavor and tastes. Chili oils use a variety of oils as a base like canola oil, olive oil, sesame oil, peanut oil and safflower oil. Using these oils give and extra depth as well as flavor to your dishes. For instance, if you wanted to accentuate only the flavor of the chili pepper combined with ginger root only, then use good canola oil. Canola oil has a neutral taste which is perfect in this case.

Infused oils can be made using the oils listed above as well. Infusing other elements like common to exotic herbs and spices, nuts and other fragrant ingredients.

THE CARIBBEAN PANTRY

- Ackees
- Aji Mirasol
- Allspice
- Ancho
- Annalto
- Avocado
- Banana Leaves
- Bananas
- Basmati Rice
- Black Beans
- Black Eye Peas
- Black Pepper
- Blood Oranges
- Bread Fruit
- Caribbean Rums
- Cassava Powder
- Celery Salt
- Cherimoyas
- Chili Powder
- Chilies (Dried)
- Chilies (Fresh)
- Chipolte
- Cilantro
- Congo Pepper
- Corn
- Cinnamon
- Coconut
- Coriander
- Cumin
- Curry
- Curry Leaves
- Curry Powder
- Figs
- Fresno
- Garam Masala
- Ginger
- Grapefruit
- Guajillo
- Guava
- Habanero Chili Peppers
- Hot Pepper Sauces
- Jalapenos
- Jamaica Hot
- Jasmine Rice
- Jerk Seasoning
- Jicama
- Lemons
- Limes
- Mangos
- Mint
- Mulatto
- Nutmeg
- Okra
- Papaya
- Paprika
- Pasada
- Passion Fruit
- Pequin
- Pineapple
- Pinto Beans
- Plantains
- Poblanos
- Prickly Peas
- Pumpkin
- Rice
- Rum
- Serranos Chili Peppers
- Scotch Bonnets Chili Peppers
- Sweet Peppers
- Sweet Potatoes
- White Pepper
- Yams

MEATS

Beef	Goat
Chicken	Pork
Game	Veal

FISH AND SEAFOOD

Abalone	Mahi Mahi	Sea Urchin
Ahi Tuna	Mussels	Shrimp
Clams	Oysters	Spiny Lobster
Conch	Pompano	Sword Fish
Crab	Red Snapper	Trout
Grouper	Salt Cod	Yellow Tail Tuna
Lobster	Scallops	
Mackerel	Sea Bass	

THE TROPICAL ASIAN PANTRY

Bamboo Shoots	Ginger Juice	Red Curry Paste
Basil	Grapefruit	Sake
Bean Thread Noodles	Green Curry Paste	Sambal Sekera
Beni Shoga	Hoisin Sauce	Shichimi (7 Spices)
Bok Choy	Japanese Cucumbers	Shitaki Mushrooms
Chili Paste	Kaffir Limes	Soy Sauce
Chinese Cucumbers	Lemongrass	Star Anise
Cilantro	Lemons	Star Fruit
Citrus Fruits	Limes	Szechwan Pepper
Coconut Milk	Mangos	Tamarind
Coconuts	Mirin	Thai Basil
Curry Spices	Miso	Thai Chili Peppers
Daikon	Oranges	Wasabi
Enoki Mushrooms	Papaya	Water Chestnuts
Galangal	Pickled Ginger	Yellow Curry Paste
Garam Masala	Pineapple	5 Spice Powder
Ginger	Plum Paste	

MEATS

Beef	Goat
Chicken	Pork
Game	Veal

FISH AND SEAFOOD

Abalone	Mahi Mahi	Sea Urchin
Ahi Tuna	Mussels	Shrimp
Clams	Oysters	Spiny Lobster
Conch	Pompano	Sword Fish
Crab	Red Snapper	Trout
Grouper	Salt Cod	Yellow Tail
Tuna		
Lobster	Scallops	
Mackerel	Sea Bass	

Please note I like to incorporate wines and liqueurs as another element. And flavoring into my signature recipe creations my recipes can also be made without them if. You choose to omit them the recipes will still come out bursting with flavor and they will be very exciting and tasty. Also some of liqueurs that I use in the recipes can be ordered online just go to their web site.

CONTENTS

Appetizers

New Groove Fuszion Style Onion Rings 2
New Groove Clams and Oysters Casino
    Laced with Champagne and Cognac 4
New Groove Fuszion Spicy Stuffed Mussels on the Half Shell 6
The Chef's Grilled Vegetable Medley 7
Mini Seafood Cakes With Crab, Shrimp and Crawfish 8
Spicy New Groove Chicken Liver Toast 10
New Groove Fusion Crostini 11
New Groove Super Spiced Shrimp "Take" 1 12
New Groove Salzbrezein Pretzels 13
New Groove Fusion Buttermilk Bisciuts 15

Soups

New Groove Double Nickle Soul Brother Buffalo Chili 18
New Groove House Funk Chili With Beer, Tequila, Rum, Bourbon 20
New Groove Oyster And Scallop Chowder 22
Sarah Paretti & Stacy Walther Roasted Chicken Corn
    Chowder Top with Bacon with a Soul Brother Take on it 24
New Groove Fusion Surf N Turf Chowder 26
Hot Chili Sausage and Shrimp Soup Laced
    With Cognac, and Rum 28
New Groove Cream of Chicken Soup
    With Cognac and Roasted Corn 30
"Off The Hook" Manhattan Clam Chowder 32
New Groove Fusion Lamb Stew 34
New Groove Crab, Lobster, Oyster Vegetable Soup 36
Lobster, Shrimp, Tomato Pasta Soup 38
New Groove Ginger Pork Soup With Mango 39

New Groove Fusion Fruit Soup 40
New Groove Chicken-Ginger Crawfish Soup 41
New Groove Shrimp, Chicken, Corn Tortilla Soup.............................. 42

Stocks and Sauces

New Groove Chicken Stock 46
New Groove Beef Stock 47
New Groove Veal Stock 48
New Groove Fish Stock 49
New Groove Seafood Stock 50
New Groove Vegetable Stock 51
New Groove Turkey Stock..52
New Groove Fusion Vegetable Stock..53

Salads & Greens

New Groove Vegetable Saute Asparagus 56
Slick Rick's Roasted Vegetable Jackpot Over Roasted
    Spaghetti Squash..57
Creamy Honey-Lime Citrus Dressing
    Laced With Tequila and Rum 59
New Groove Mediterranean Salad.. 60
New Groove Plantain Fruit Salad 62
New Groove Caesar Salad Gone Wild 64
Chef Signature Recipe New Groove Rhapsody Salad........................65
New Groove Carrot Salad With Figs And Dates.................................67
New Groove Pasta Salad With Tuna And Vegetables.......................69
Chef Signature Recipe New Groove Crab and Shrimp Slaw..............71
New Groove Crab, Scallop Tomato Seafood Salad............................73
New Groove Salad With Vinaigrette Dressing....................................75
New Groove Roasted Eggplant And Pepper Salad............................76
New Groove Pasta Salad..78

New Groove French Style Green Beans...80
New Groove Fusion Baked Acorn Squash..81
New Groove Broccoli Rabe With Black Walnuts And Champagne....82
New Groove Fusion Glazed Baby Carrots..83
New Groove Mustard Greens With Cabbage 'Take' 1.........................84
New Groove Okra, Corn, Tomatoes With Peppers, Onions...............85
New Groove Green Beans 86
New Groove Ratatouille Saute...87

Rice & Pasta Other Starches

New Groove Chicken N Pasta Twisted..90
New Groove Pasta With Lobster And Chicken 92
New Groove Risotto Twisted 94
New Groove Roasted Yukon Gold Potatoes.. 95
New Groove Seafood Bolognese...96
New Groove Seafood Saute Over Saffron Pasta 97
Chef Rick's New Groove Orzo Medley..98
New Groove Buttermilk, Garlic, Cheese Mashed
    Potatoes 'Take' 1 100
New Groove Fusion Wild Rice 'Take' 1 101
New Groove Wild Mushroom And Wild Rice 102
Chef Gant's "Groovin" Rice Pilaf... 103
Chef Gant's New Groove Stuffed Twice Baked Potatoes................ 104
Chef Rick's Perfect Pasta With Seafood and Tomatoes.................... 105
Pasta With Shrimp, Sausage and Shitaki Mushrooms....................... 107
Orzo With Chili's, Onions, Peas and Prosciutto..................................... 109
Pasta With Lobster, Crab, Shrimp, Sausage And Mushrooms........ 111
Curried Rice With Ginger, Peppers, Beef, and Shrimp........................113
Roasted White Corn and Red Beans
    With Jalapeno and Anaheim Chile Pepper Rice
    Laced with Cognac Rum and Tequila..115
Roasted White Corn And Red Beans With Habenero Rice
    Laced With Coconut Rum And Peppar Vodka 117

New Groove Pizza Dough 118
Spicy Fusion-Style Italian Breadsticks 119
New Groove Pizza Sauce 121
New Groove Pizza Dough 2 122
New Groove Sausage and Mushroom Pizza 123
New York Style New Groove Pizza 125
New Groove Surf N Turf Pizza 126
Turkey Sausage Pizza With Blue Cheese, Jalapeno's
    and Serrano Peppers 127

Main Dishes

East - West Style Stuffed Chicken Breast 132
New Groove Chicken N Peaches Twisted 134
New Groove Stuffed Pork Chops 136
New Groove Veal Medalions Twisted 138
Fusion Style Spicy Steak Portuguese
    Laced With Tequila and Bourbon 140
Grilled Rib Eye Steaks with a Garlic, Mustard Sauce 142
New York Strip Steaks With a Thai Marinade Fusion Style 144
New Groove Fusion Tangerine Steak 146
New Groove Firey Steak Provencale 147
Crazy Zanzibar Fusion New York Strip Steaks
    With Grand Marnier and Citron Vodka 149
New York Strip Steak And Shrimp Hook-Up Done
    New Groove Style 151
Moroccan Style New Groove Steaks
    With Cognac and Calvados 152
Sauteed Chicken Breast With Almonds, Hazelnuts and Plums 154
Spicy-Hot Ginger-Citrus, Chicken and Shrimp
    Laced With Ginger Brandy and Pineapple Rum 156
Pan Seared Chicken Breast With Broccoli and Fusilli Pasta 158
New Groove Style Pan Seared Chicken Breasts
    With Black Olives, Garlic and Champagne Over Penne 160

Chef Gant's Mango-Orange Sauteed Chicken Breasts
    With Mango Rum and Mandarin Vodka.. 161
Saute Chicken Thighs With Crab, Conch and Chili Peppers........... 163
New Groove Miami Style Citrus Chicken 165
Caribbean Pork Medallions With Coconut And Chili Peppers 167
Wild Mushrooms And Garlic Over Sauted Pork Medallions........... 169
Grilled Pork Medallions With Glazed Apples And Pears 170
Flavorful Grilled Pork Medallions With a Spicy Roasted
    Yellow Pepper Sauce with Tequila, Peppar Vodka and
    Champagne.. 172
Roast Pork Tenderloin With Fresh Herbs New Groove Style 174
Sauted Pork Medallions With Plum Tomatoes, Italian Hot
    Peppers, Red Onions, Black Olives Laced with Cognac,
    Black Rum and Champagne... 175
New Groove Fusion Pork Cordon Bleu
    With a Lemon Rum Caper Sauce... 177
Spicy Veal Saltimbocca
    With a Plum Tomato Champagne Rum Sauce 179
Veal Medalions With Apples, Dates, Pine Nuts and
    French Apple Brandy.. 181
Veal Medalions With Black Olives, Tomatoes, and Artichokes....... 183
Chef Signature Recipe Saute Veal Cutlet's With Wild
    Mushrooms, Tarragon, Oregano, Champagne and Rum 185
Breaded Veal Cutlets With a Champagne,
    Tarragon Cream Sauce.. 187
Marinade Grilled Veal Chops and Lime Citrus Sauce........................ 189
Stuffed Veal Chop With A Cranberry Pear Sauce................................ 191

Fish & Seafood...

Slickrick's Salmon Marsala Over Rice... 194
Blackened Chilean Sea Bass Filets With a Citrus Bourbon Sauce..... 196
Three Green Pasta With Scallops, Sea Bass, Lobster,
    And Rock Shrimp 198

Grilled Halibut Filets With A Spicy Maple Rum Sauce 200
New Groove Fuszion Pappardelle Sugo Pomoboro D'Mari 202
New Groove Style Shrimp Scampi 204
New Groove Fish H' Raimi 206
Curried Lobster Shrimp Pilau Fusion Style 208
Caribbean Style Crab And Crawfish Over Rice 210
The Seafood "Fusion" Hookup 212
Fettuccine With Shrimp, Grouper, Orange Roughy
    And Tomatoes 214
Jumbo Shrimp With Jumbo Lump Crab Meat Cognac,
    Rum And Champagne 216
East-West Style Seafood Creole 218
Cornmeal Crusted Trout With Citrus Pecan Hazelnut Butter 220
New Groove Seafood Cioppino 222

Chutneys and Salsas

Lobster, Shrimp And Scallop Curry With Tropical Salsa 226
Moroccan-Caribbean Duo Fusion Salsa 228
Grilled Mango Fusion Chutney 229
Asian Fire Chutney Laced With Ginger Brandy and
    Peppar Vodka 230
Shotgun Caribbean Salsa Laced With Ginger Brandy and Rum ... 231
Cucumber-Bermuda Onion Ginger Salsa 232
Grilled Mango With Fusion Chutney 233
New Groove House Style Fusion Salsa 234

Sweets, Desserts and Sweets Desserts

Fuszion Style Madeleines 236
New Groove Fuszion Style Pound Cake 238
New Groove Blackberry and Raspberry Short-Cake 239
Fuszion Style Tiramisu 241

New Groove Peach Mango Shortcake
   With A Orange Custard Sauce 243
New Groove Chocolate Cold Sweat Shortcake 245
New Groove Bread Pudding With Dates Nuts and Cranberries ... 248
New Groove Cherry Cobbler With Rum Cherry Brandy
   and Champagne 250
New Groove Ginger Champagne Lemon Cake 252
New Groove Triple Chocolate Chip Bar Cookies 254
New Groove Amaretto Cheese Cookies 256
New Groove Fruit Cobbler With Peach Schnapps And Rum 257
New Groove French Apple Pie With Applejack Brandy 259
New Groove Chocolate Apple Zucchini Cake 261
New Groove Anisette Toast 263
New Groove Banana Fosters Cookies 264
New Groove Key Lime Pie Laced With Tequila Dark Rum
   and Limon Rum With a Vanilla Rum Tequila Whipped
   Cream Topping 266
New Groove Ginger Apricot Cookies 268
New Groove Orange Pineapple Cup Cakes 269
New Groove Coconut and Pineapple Cream Pie 271
New Groove Caribbean Carrot Cake 'Take' 1 273
New Groove Coconut and Banana Cream Pie 275
New Groove Chocolate Chip Cookies with Bourbon and Rum 277
The Cold Sweat Apple Shortcake 278
New Groove Fuszion Style Pecan Pie With Chocolate W/
   Vanilla Rum Bourbon, Black Rum, 151 Rum, Apple Jack
   Brandy 281
New Groove Banana Fosters Cookies "Take" 2 282

Cold & Delicious Beverages

New Groove Orange and Peach Lemonade 286
New Groove Pineapple and Peach Lemonade 287
New Groove Fruit Smoothie Gone Wild 288

Strawberry Cooler Lemonade 289
Strawberry and Raspberry Lemonade 290
New Groove Three Berry Lemonade..291
New Groove Strawberry Peach Smoothie..292
New Groove Strawberry and Raspberry Lemonade 293
New Groove Strawberry Cooler Lemonade...294

Seasonings & Rubs

New Groove Asian 5 Spice Powder..297
New Groove Caribbean Spice Powder...298
New Groove Island Spice Powder..299
New Groove Asian-Caribbean Spice Powder......................................300
New Groove Southwest/Mexican Spice Powder 301
New Groove Southern/Cajun Spice Powder.......................................302
New Groove Italian/Mediterranean Seasoning..................................303
New Groove House Seasoning 1 304
New Groove House Seasoning II 305
Chef Rick's Seasoning Blend..306
New Groove "Dragon's Heat" Seasoning Blend..................................307
Chef Rick's New Groove All-Purpose Fusion Rub...............................308
New Groove Grill Blends I...309
New Groove Grill Blends II 310
New Groove Grill Blends III..311

Appetizers

Appetizers and Finger Foods...

The perfect appetizers can set the for your lunch and dinner that is why I specifically selected the following recipes from my best of the recipe collection if you want to entice. Your taste buds for what lies ahead then start with one of my delicious flavor explosive appetizers. They are perfect prelude to a fusion inspired dinning experience.

NEW GROOVE FUSZION STYLE ONION RINGS

- 2 Large Red Onions peeled sliced ⅜ inch thick
- 2 Large Vidalia Onions peeled sliced ⅜ inch thick
- 5 cups All-purpose Flour season with new Groove House Seasoning I or Kosher salt and coarse ground black pepper
- 4 cups of canola oil for cooking onion rings
- 8 cups fresh bread crumbs
- 3 Tablespoons crushed red pepper flakes
- 3 Tablespoons New Groove House Seasoning I
- 2 cups Grated Italian Blend Cheese ¼ cup fresh chopped Chervil
- 3 Tablespoons Fresh Thai Basil chopped
- 3 Tablespoons Fresh Lemon Thyme
- 2 Tablespoons Ground Cinnamon
- 2 Tablespoons Ground Nutmeg For Batter
- 3 Jumbo eggs
- ¼ cup fresh chopped garlic cloves
- 4 Tablespoons fresh Ginger chopped
- 4 cups All-Purpose Flour
- 2 ½ to 3 cups Buttermilk ¼ cup Champagne
- ¼ cup Hennessey cognac ¼ cup Bacardi Black Rum
- ¼ cup Laird's Apple Jack Brandy

Procedure:

First in a large mixing bowl combine eggs buttermilk, champagne, black rum, cognac, apple jack brandy stir to a blend then add your flour. Ginger, garlic mix until smooth. Then in another large mixing bowl add your Flour New Groove House Seasoning I or kosher salt and coarse ground black pepper. Then in another large mixing bowl combine Fresh bread crumbs, Italian blend cheese, New Groove House seasoning I, crushed Red pepper Flakes, Chervil, Thai Basil. Lemon Thyme, Ground Cinnamon, Ground nutmeg then stir to blend. Then dredge your sliced onion rings in seasoned flour, then dip in Batter, then roll in seasoned bread crumbs. Then in a large 8 qt Dutch oven over medium high heat then add your canola oil then drop your onion rings in the hot oil cook onion rings in batches for about 3 minutes or until golden brown then drain on paper towels then serve.

NEW GROOVE CLAMS AND OYSTERS CASINO
LACED WITH CHAMPAGNE AND COGNAC

Serves 5 to 6

Ingredients:

36	cherry stone little-neck clams on the half-shell
36	oysters on the half-shell
2	sticks sweet butter
1	medium-size green pepper, finely chopped
1	medium-size yellow pepper, finely chopped
1	medium-size red pepper, finely chopped
1	medium-size red onion, finely chopped ¼ cup fresh parsley, chopped
¼	cup Hennessey Cognac ¼ cup champagne
10	strips smoked bacon, cooked, drained, crumbled
1	lb sweet sausage, casing removed, cooked, crumbled
2	Jalapeno peppers, seeded and finely chopped
2	habenero peppers, seeded and finely chopped
1	tbsp fresh ginger, finely chopped
1	tbsp fresh garlic, finely chopped Salt and white pepper to taste
	Season with New Groove House Seasoning

Procedure:

Preheat oven to 375ºF. In large skillet over medium heat, add butter, then peppers, onion, parsley, cognac, champagne. Sauté for 4 minutes, then remove from heat. Transfer to a medium-size bowl, let cool. Then spoon mixture on to clams and oysters, then top oysters and clams with bacon and sausage, and then bake oysters and clams on a baking sheet at 375º for about 7 minutes. Serve hot!

NEW GROOVE FUSZION SPICY STUFFED MUSSELS ON THE HALF SHELL

- 2 lbs Hot Italian sausage casings remove cooked then crumbled
- 3 cups bread brumbs
- 3 Jalapeno chili peppers seeded finely chopped
- 3 Thai Chili peppers seeded finely chopped
- 3 Tablespoons fresh flat leaf parsley chopped
- 3 Tablespoons fresh garlic cloves chopped
- 3 plum tomatoes medium diced
- 2 jumbo eggs
- 1/3 cup Jim Beam black bourbon
- 1/3 cup Myers's rum original dark Jamaican rum
- 3 Tablespoons Olive oil
  Season to taste with Kosher salt and coarse ground black pepper
- 3 lbs Green Lip Mussels
- 4 cups water to cook Mussels

Procedure:

In a large mixing bowl add your sausage eggs ½ cup bread crumbs, tomatoes thai chili peppers and Jalapeno chili peppers, parsley, garlic, Rum Bourbon mix well then season to taste with Kosher salt and coarse ground black pepper then put aside then in large 8 qt Dutch oven over high heat add your water then mussels bring to a boil cover and cook for 10 minutes or until mussels open then remove from heat then loosen meat from shell leave in shell then place mussels on a baking sheet then divide the sausage mixture among the mussels then sprinkle with the rest of the bread crumbs then bake at 375°F for 8 minutes then remove from oven.

Serve hot!

THE CHEF'S GRILLED VEGETABLE MEDLEY

Makes 6 servings

Ingredients:

- 5 medium carrots peeled and sliced ¼" thick
- 2 medium Zucchini sliced ¼" thick
- 2 medium yellow squash sliced ¼" thick
- 1 medium Vidalia onion sliced ¼" thick
- 1 medium Bermuda onion, sliced ¼" thick
- 6 Ears Sweet Yellow corn, Grilled then cut off cob
- 5 medium Italian hot peppers, cut in half then seeded
- 5 medium Serrano Hot Peppers cut in Half then seeded
- 3 cups wild mushrooms

Marinade:

- 1 ¼ cups olive oil
- 1 cup fresh basil leaf, chopped fine ½ cup fresh cilantro, chopped fine ½ cup fresh rosemary, chopped fine ⅓ cup white wine optional
- ½ cup fresh garlic cloves roasted in olive oil ¼ cup fresh ginger root chopped fine
- 3 cups black olives pitted

  Season to taste with salt and white pepper

Procedure:

In a food processor combine all ingredients for marinade ginger and garlic and blend smooth transfer to a large bowl add vegetables and toss to coat well. Transfer to hot grill. Grill 3 to 4 minutes per side then remove and arrange on a large plate and serve hot.

MINI SEAFOOD CAKES WITH CRAB, SHRIMP AND CRAWFISH

Makes 8 servings

Ingredients:

- 1   16 oz package crawfish meat chopped
- 1   lb can jumbo lump crab meat
- 1   lb 16/20 jumbo shrimp cleaned and chopped
- 10   cups Italian bread crumbs
- 3   jumbo eggs
- ¼   cup flat leaf parsley chopped
- ¼   cup djion mustard
- ½   cup mayo
- 2   tablespoons Worcestershire sauce
- 2 ½ tablespoons new groove house seasoning 2
- 1   small red onion peeled and small diced
- 1   medium size red bell pepper seeded and chopped
- 4   medium size jalapeno chili peppers seeded and chopped
- ¼   cup absolut vanilla vodka
- ¼   cup jose Cuervo gold tequia
- ¼   cup Myers's Dark Rum

Season to taste with kosher salt and coarse ground black pepper

Procedure:

First pre-heat oven to 375°F in a large mixing bowl combine Italian bread crumbs, jumbo eggs, flat leaf parsley, mustard, mayo, Worcestershire sauce, red onion, red bell pepper, jalapeno chili peppers, new groove house seasoning 2, dark rum, gold tequila, vanilla vodka, jumbo lump crab meat, crawfish tail meat, jumbo shrimp. Then mix well then season to taste with kosher salt and coarse ground black pepper then form small ball then flatten into cakes and place onto non-stick-baking . Then place into oven then bake at 375*F for 5 to 7 minutes then remove seafood cakes from oven then place on serving platter then serve.

SPICY NEW GROOVE CHICKEN LIVER TOAST

Makes 6 servings

Ingredients:

1 ½	lbs chicken livers
⅓	cup olive oil
1	tablespoon crushed red pepper flakes
4	medium Serrano peppers, seeded and diced
2	tablespoons fresh garlic, finely chopped
2	tablespoons fresh ginger, finely chopped
¼	cup white wine
¼	cup Bacardi dark rum
1	cup chicken stock
⅓	cup fresh cilantro, chopped
2	medium French bread baguettes, sliced ½" thick
	Salt and white pepper, to taste

Procedure:

Slice the livers into fairly large pieces. In a large Dutch oven over medium high heat, add olive oil, red pepper flakes, garlic, chicken livers, wine, chicken stock, rum and Serrano peppers. Cook for 15 minutes and season to taste with salt and pepper. Remove from heat and transfer to food processor. Blend until smooth. Transfer to bowl and let cool. Preheat oven to 350°F then add bread slices and brush lightly with olive oil and bake until golden brown and remove from oven then spread the chicken liver mixture on toast and then serve garnish with fresh chopped Cilantro and crushed red pepper flakes.

NEW GROOVE FUSION CROSTINI

Makes 5 servings

Ingredients:
- 1 cup kalamata olive-pitted
- ¼ cup olive oil
- ¼ cup pecans, toasted
- ¼ cup pine nuts, toasted
- 1 small onion, diced small
- 5 medium Thai Chilie peppers, fire roasted, seeded and chopped
- ¼ cup Hennessy Cognac ¼ cup fresh garlic, chopped
- 2 medium yellow bell peppers, seeded and diced
- 1 large French bread baguette, sliced ½" thick
- Salt and white pepper to taste

Procedure:

In a food processor combine olives, pine nuts, pecans, olive oil, cognac, onion, garlic and peppers. Blend until smooth. Preheat oven to 350°F. Place bread slices onto non-stick baking sheet and lightly brush with olive oil. Bake until golden. Remove and top off with mixture and serve hot. Garnish with toasted pine nuts and finely diced yellow bell peppers.

NEW GROOVE
SUPER SPICED SHRIMP "TAKE" 1

Makes 4 servings

Ingredients:
- ½ cup horseradish, mix together
- ⅓ cup olive oil, mix together
- ⅓ cup Worcestershire sauce, mix together
- ¼ cup Hennessey cognac, mix together
- 2 tablespoons Tabasco sauce, mix together
- 2 qt water
- 2 12 oz bottle corona beer
- 3 medium scotch bonnets peppers, seeded and chopped
- 4 cloves fresh garlic, peeled
- 4 tablespoons yellow mustard seeds
- 3 medium bay leaves
- 2 lbs 16/20 jumbo shrimp, peeled and deveined
- 3 medium lemons, sliced thin
- 2 tablespoons salt
- 2 to 3 cups Bacardi Gold Rum
- 2 to 3 Tablespoons of Old Bay Seasoning

Procedure:

First mix the first 5 ingredients in a large bowl, cover and let stand at room temp. Then in a large 8 qt Dutch oven over high heat add old bay water, garlic mustard seeds scotch bonnets, beer, and rum and bring to a boil. Then reduce heat to Medium and cook for 10 minutes. Then add shrimp, lemons, bay leaves salt and cook for 5 minutes then strain the shrimp add the shrimp to the horseradish mixture stir to blend set aside to cool. Serve at room temp.

Serve with your favorite crusty bread and cheese

NEW GROOVE
SALZBREZEIN PRETZELS

Makes 12 servings

Ingredients:

4	teaspoons dry yeast, mixed with water
¾	cups water
1 ¾	cups all-purpose flour
2	teaspoons salt, mix with flour
⅓	cup cilantro, finely chopped
⅓	cup Bacardi gold rum add to water
⅓	cup Absolut vanilla vodka add to water
⅓	fresh Thai Chilie peppers, seeded finely chop
2	fresh Serrano peppers, seeded finely chop
2	fresh red jalapeno Chilie peppers, seeded finely chop
⅓	cup Monterey jack cheese, grated
⅓	cup parmesan reggiano cheese, grated
2	jumbo eggs, beaten
3	tablespoons water, mix together
	Sesame seeds, toppings for pretzel
	Poppy seeds, toppings for pretzel
	Kosher salt, toppings for pretzel

Procedure:

First in a small bowl add a ½ cup water then sprinkle in the yeast leave for 5 minutes stir to dissolve then in large bowl add flour, salt, cilantro

Thai Chilie peppers, Serrano Chilie peppers, red jalapeno Chilie peppers, Monterey jack cheese, parmesan reggiano cheese stir to blend then make a well in the center

And pour in the dissolved yeast. Use a wooden spoon to draw enough of the flour into the dissolved yeast to form a soft paste cover the bowl with a dish towel

And let sponge until frothy and risen about 20 minutes then mix in the flour stir in the vanilla vodka, gold rum, and remaining water as needed to form stiff sticky dough.

Turn the dough out onto a lightly floured work surface knead until smooth and elastic about 10 minutes then put the dough in a bowl and cover with a dish towel.

Let rise until doubled in size 1 ½-2 hours punch down, then let rest for 10 minutes then divide the dough into 12 pieces shape each piece into a round roll and then

Into an oval roll each oval backward and forward with your fingers along the dough until it forms a strip about 16 inches long and thick in the middle.

Once the dough has been divided and shaped into strips pick up the two ends of each strip to make a loop cross the ends over twice and then press them down

On either side of the dough then. Repeat with each strip of dough place the pretzels on a lightly floured baking sheet and cover with a dish towel proof

Until each piece has doubled in size about 45 minutes in small bowl beat two eggs mixed with water to make egg glaze. Then pre heat oven at 425°F then brush

The egg glaze over each pretzel and sprinkle with toppings of your choice. Bake at 425°F for 15 to 20 minutes until golden brown. Then remove pretzels from oven then place pretzels in a basket then serve with mustard.

NEW GROOVE FUSION BUTTERMILK BISCIUTS

Makes 1 dozen biscuits

Ingredients:
- 4 ½ cups all-purpose flour
- 2 ½ tsp baking powder, add to flour
- 1 tsp salt, add to flour
- ½ tsp ground allspice
- ½ tsp chili powder
- 1 ½ tsp curry powder
- 1 ½ tsp baking soda, add to flour
- 2 sticks sweet butter, softened
- 1 cup granulated sugar
- ⅓ cup honey
- 3 jumbo eggs
- ⅓ cup French apple brandy (calvados)
- ⅓ cup Bacardi gold rum
- 1 cup buttermilk
- ½ cup coconut milk
- 1 tbsp lemon zest
- 1 tbsp orange zest
- 1 tsp lemon grass, grated
- 1 cup dried dates, finely chopped
- 1 cup coconut flakes, toasted
- ¼ cup candied ginger, finely minced

Procedure:

Preheat oven at 400°F.

Mixture 1:

Blend the sugar, honey and sweet butter together then add in your sifted flour, salt, baking soda, baking powder, then add coconut flakes Lemon zest. Orange zest, lemon grass, dates, candied ginger, all-spice, chili powder, curry powder mix well.

Mixture 2:

In a separate bowl add your buttermilk, coconut milk eggs, French apple brandy, gold rum. Beat with a wire whisk until blended. Gradually add the second mixture to your first and blend. Once both mixtures have been blended the dough may seem on the dry side. If so, incorporate additional buttermilk to loosen a bit then pinch off 1 inch to 1 ½ inch dough portions. Lightly dust with flour. Place dough portions on a greased sheet pan and bake for 15 to 20 minutes. Then remove biscuits from oven and place in a basket to serve with breakfast or dinner.

Soups

Soups & Chowders & Chilis...

Often soups, chowders, and chili were thought of as the poor man's dinner well times have change. They can range in a variety of types from condensed to sublime to homemade. I offer a wide and vast variety to choose from you can go to mild to wild and they are all satisfying anytime.

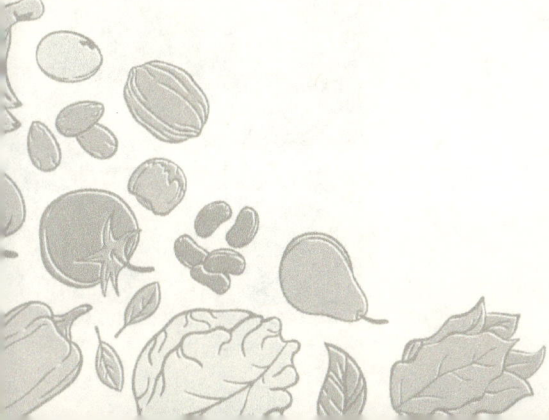

NEW GROOVE DOUBLE NICKLE SOUL BROTHER BUFFALO CHILI

Ricky Gant copyrighted 2011

Makes 8 servings.

- 6 lbs ground buffalo meat, cooked and drained
- 2 medium red onions, peeled and chopped
- 3 medium leeks, cleaned and sliced
- 2 fresh serrano peppers, seeded and chopped
- 2 fresh long hot chili peppers, seeded and chopped
- 2 fresh jalapeno chili peppers, seeded and chopped
- 2 fresh Habanero chile pepper, seeded and chopped
- 2 fresh Italian peppers, seeded and chopped
- 2 fresh Anaheim chili peppers, seeded and chopped
- 2 28 oz crushed tomatoes
- 1 28 oz can diced tomatoes
- 2 15 oz cans dark red kidney beans, rinsed and drained
- 2 15 oz cans black beans, rinsed and drained
- 1 bunch fresh cilantro, chopped
- 1 bunch fresh flat-leaf parsley, chopped
- 2 teaspoons ground cinnamon
- 2 teaspoons ground allspice
- 2 teaspoons ground nutmeg
- 2 teaspoons crushed red pepperflakes
- 2 teaspoons cayenne pepper
- 2 teaspoons ground cumin
- 2 teaspoons chili powder
- 2 teaspoons coarse ground black pepper
- 4 teaspoons kosher salt

- ⅓ cup dark brown sugar
- 2 cups water
- ½ cup safflower
- ¼ cup fresh orange juice
- ¼ cup fresh grapefruit juice
- ¼ cup Hennessey black cognac
- ¼ cup laird's apple jack brandy
- ¼ cup gosling's black seal rum
- ¼ cup jose cuervo tequila
- ¼ cup johnnie walker red scotch
- ¼ cup jim beam devil's cut bourbon
- ¼ cup absolut vodka
- ¼ cup absolut peppar vodka

Procedure:

First in a large 8 Quart Dutch Oven over medium heat add your safflower oil then add your buffalo meat cook until brown then remove from heat drained your buffalo meat. Then add meat back to your dutch oven over medium heat. Then add your crushed tomatoes, diced Tomatoes, red onions, leeks, italian peppers, All your chili peppers water kidney beans, black beans, cilantro, flat leaf parsley, ground cinnamon ground nutmeg, ground all-spice, crushed red pepper flakes, cayenne pepper, ground cumin, chili powder, coarse ground black pepper, kosher salt, dark brown sugar, orange juice, grapefruit juice, black cognac, apple jack brandy, black rum, tequila, scotch, bourbon, vodka, peppar vodka stir. Then simmer for one hour. Then taste adjust seasonings. Then remove from heat serve in bowls. Serves 8 people.

Makes about 3 gallons of Buffalo Chili.

Serve in Bowls.

NEW GROOVE HOUSE FUNK CHILI WITH BEER, TEQUILA, RUM, BOURBON

R. Gant copyrighted 2011 & 2012

Makes 7 servings.

2	lbs ground turkey
2	lbs ground chicken
2	medium Vidalia onions, peeled and diced
2	fresh long hot green peppers, seeded and chopped
5	fresh jalapeno chili pepper, seeded and chopped
2	fresh Italian peppers, seeded and chopped
2	fresh Hungarian hot peppers, seeded and chopped
1	bunch fresh cilantro, chopped
2	15 oz cans white kidney beans, drained and rinse
2	15 oz cans red kidney beans, drained and rinse
2	15 oz cans black beans, drained and rinse
2	28 oz cans crushed tomatoes
2	cups water
2 ½	tablespoons crushed red pepper flakes
2 ½	tablespoons cayenne pepper
2	tablespoons ground coriander
2	tablespoons ground sage
2	tablespoons ground cumin
2	tablespoons chili powder
2	tablespoons ground black pepper
4	tablespoons kosher salt
3 ½	tablespoons sugar
¼	cup fresh lemon juice
1	8 oz bottle coronia beer
½	cup jim beam devil's cut bourbon

½ cup Don Q 151 Rum
½ cup jose cuervo tequila
½ cup Canola oil

Procedure:

First in a large 8qt Dutch oven over medium heat add your canola oil then ground turkey and ground chicken break up meat with a wooden spoon stir cook meat for 15 minutes then drain your meat back to the Dutch oven over medium low heat then add your kosher salt, sage, coriander, ground black pepper, cayenne pepper, crushed red pepper flakes, cumin, chili pepper, sugar, crushed tomatoes, water, Vidalia onions, Italian peppers, hot long green peppers, jalapeno chili peppers, hungarian peppers, black beans, red kidney beans, white kidney beans, cilantro, lemon juice, beer, bourbon, 151 rum, tequila then stir chili simmer for one hour then taste adjust seasonings to taste. Then remove from heat serve with white brown rice makes about 2 gallons of chili serves 7.

Per serving (excluding unknown items): 82935 Calories; 30.1g Fat (32.0% calories from fat); 57.5g Protien; 86.8g Carbohydrate; 112mg Cholesterol; 3396mg sodium. Exchanges: 5 Grains(Starch); 6 Lean Meat; 1 Vegetable; ½ Fruit; 3 ½ Fat; ½ Other Carboh.

NEW GROOVE OYSTER AND SCALLOP CHOWDER

1	large red onion, peeled and medium diced
4	medium carrots peeled and medium diced
4	medium celery medium diced
4	large Yukon gold potatoes medium diced
3	dozen bay scallops
3	dozen oysters cleaned chopped
3	tablespoon fresh flat parsley spring chopped
1	medium bay leaf
2	spring fresh thyme
6	cups chicken stock or seafood stock
3	tablespoons sweet butter
8	strips bacon cooked and drained
3	cups buttermilk
3	cups heavy whipping cream
4	tablespoon all-purpose flour for oysters
1 ¼	cups French apple brandy (calvades)
1 ¼	cups champagne
1	teaspoon fresh orange zest garnish
1	teaspoon fresh lime zest garnish
1	teaspoon fresh lemon zest garnish
	Kosher salt and ground white pepper to taste

Procedure:

In a large 8 quart dutch oven over medium heat sauté bacon until fat has been rendered and bacon is crisp then the fat then stir in your chicken stock or seafood stock. Then cook for 5 minutes then add potatoes carrots, celery, red onions stir cook for 10 to 12 minutes or until tender then reduce to simmer then add your French apple brandy, champagne. Buttermilk, heavy whipping cream, sweet butter, flour oysters, bay scallops, parsley, thyme, bay leaf then stir until blended then simmer additional 20 minutes then season to taste with kosher salt and ground white pepper and then remove from heat and put chowder into bowl and remove bay leaf before serving garnish with lemon, lime, orange zest.

SARAH PARETTI & STACY WALTHER ROASTED CHICKEN CORN CHOWDER TOP WITH BACON WITH A SOUL BROTHER TAKE ON IT

5	lbs boneless chicken breast cleaned and seasoned with kosher salt and coarse ground black pepper then roast at 375°F let cool then medium dice
2	lbs bag carrots peeled and sliced
1	bunch fresh celery cleaned and sliced
3	packs fresh corn on the cob cut off the cob
1	bunch Fresh leeks cleaned and sliced
1	bunch fresh parsnips peeled and sliced
1	bunch fresh flat leaf parsley or 1 bunch fresh cilantro chopped
2	quarts vegetable stock or chicken stock
1 to 2	pounds applewood smoked bacon cooked at 375°F then drain on paper towels then chop then diced
4	pounds red blist potatoes or Yukon gold potatoes
1 ⅓	cups Canola oil
1 ⅓	cups All-Purpose Flour add to vegetables to make Roux
2 to 3	cups Champagne
½ to 1	cup Absolut Peppar Vodka
½ to 1	cup Bourbon Whiskey
½ to 1	cup Apple Jack Brandy
1 to 2	Tablespoons crushed red pepper flakes
1 to 2	Tablespoons Ground White Pepper
1	quart heavy whipping cream
½	galllon half & half
	Kosher salt to taste

Procedure:

First pre-heat your oven at 375°F then place. Your chicken breast on a large baking sheet season with kosher salt and coarse ground black pepper. Then place in oven then bake at 375°F for 27 minutes then remove chicken breast from oven let cool. Then diced your chicken breast. Then place your bacon on a large baking sheet place in oven bake at 375°F for 40 minutes then remove from oven. Then drain on paper towels let cool then chop. Then in large 12 quart stockpot over medium high heat add your canola oil. Then add your sliced carrots, celery, corn, leeks, parsnips, then stir. Cook for 9 minutes then add your flour stir cook for 4 minutes. Then add your vegetable stock or chicken stock, champagne, peppar vodka, bourbon whiskey, apple jack brandy, crushed red pepper flakes, ground white pepper, diced chicken, red blist potatoes, or Yukon gold potatoes, chopped flat leaf parsley or cilantro half & half, heavy whipping cream. Stir then reduce heat to medium then simmer for 25 minutes or until heated through. Season to taste with kosher salt then ladel chowder in bowls top with chopped bacon then serve.

NEW GROOVE FUSION SURF N TURF CHOWDER

Makes 12 servings

Ingredients:

¼	lb prosciutto ham sliced thin, then diced
½	lb apple wood smoked bacon sliced, then diced
1 ½	lbs Angus sirloin steak trimmed and sliced, then diced
6	medium Serrano peppers, seeded and diced
6	medium shallots peeled, medium diced
2	medium Vidalia onions peeled, medium diced
1	lb bag carrots peeled, medium diced
6	ears sweet yellow corn, cut off the cob
6	bunch celery, medium diced
3	medium red bliss potatoes, medium diced
1 ½	medium Yukon gold potatoes, medium diced
3	quarts milk
1 ½	quarts heavy cream
2	cups all-purpose flour, to make roux
1 ¼	cups vegetable oil, to make roux
1	cup Champagne
1 ⅓	cups Burnett vanilla vodka
1 ⅓	cups Hennessy cognac
1	bunch fresh flat-leaf parsley, chopped
1	bunch fresh tarragon, chopped
2	tablespoons crushed red pepper flakes
1	2 lb bag 16/20 jumbo shrimp cleaned and shelled, butter flied
2	1 lb package of crawfish tail meat
1	1 lb can lobster meat
1	1 lb can jumbo lump crab meat
1	1 lb can conch meat beaten to tenderize it, then diced
	Salt and white pepper, to taste

Procedure:

In a large 12 qt stock pot over medium heat add bacon, prosciutto ham, and steak then stir cook for about 12 minutes then drain off the fat then return pot to the heat

Then add your onions, shallots, garlic, chili peppers, yellow corn, celery, carrots then stir cook for 6 minutes then add vegetable oil and flour then stir well to make roux.

Then cook for 4 minutes then add your red bliss potatoes, Yukon gold potatoes, milk, heavy cream, champagne, vanilla vodka, vanilla cognac and stir well then reduce heat.

To medium low and simmer for 20 minutes then add your conch meat, crawfish tail meat, jumbo shrimp, lobster meat, jumbo lump crab meat, crushed red pepper flakes, tarragon.

Parsley then stir then simmers for another 7 minutes then season to taste with salt and white pepper then remove chowder from heat to serve chowder ladle chowder into soup bowls.

Serve with crusty bread.

HOT CHILI SAUSAGE AND SHRIMP SOUP LACED
WITH COGNAC, AND RUM

Makes 8 servings

Ingredients:

- 4 ½ quarts seafood stock or chicken stock
- 2 lb bag 16/20 jumbo shrimp cleaned, shelled, butter flied
- 3 ½ lbs sweet Italian sausage casings removed, crumbled
- 3 ½ lbs hot Italian sausage casings removed, crumbled
- 3 tablespoons fresh ginger, finely chopped
- 4 tablespoons fresh garlic cloves, finely chopped
- 4 medium Italian hot peppers, seeded and diced
- 4 medium Serrano peppers, seeded and diced
- 4 small Habanero Chile, seeded and diced
- 4 medium Jalapeno Chile peppers, seeded and diced
- 3 ears fresh yellow corn, cut off the cob
- 1 ½ lbs Italian cut green beans
- 2 medium Vidalia onions, diced small
- 2 cups Hennessey cognac
- 2 cups Bacardi dark rum 1/4 cup olive oil
- ¼ cup fresh basil, chopped fine
- 1 bunch fresh thyme
- ¼ cup fresh sage, chopped fine
- 2 cups fresh grated parmesan cheese, for garnish New groove house seasoning blend, to taste

Procedure:

In a large 8 qt Dutch oven over medium heat add olive oil then add Italian sweet sausage, and hot Italian sausage garlic, ginger, onions, corn, Italian hot peppers, and all your chili peppers

Then stir cook for 10 minutes then drain off any excess oil then add your chicken stock or seafood stock, rum, cognac, Italian cut green beans stir then simmer

For 20 minutes then add your jumbo shrimp, fresh basil, fresh thyme, fresh sage, then stir simmer for another 7 minutes then season to taste with new groove house seasoning blend

Then remove soup from heat. To serve soup ladle soup into soup bowls then garnish soup with fresh grated parmesan cheese then serve.

NEW GROOVE CREAM OF CHICKEN SOUP
WITH COGNAC AND ROASTED CORN

Makes 10 servings

Ingredients:

- 2 quarts chicken stock or low salt chicken broth
- 5 boneless skinless chicken breast medium diced
- 4 medium shallots, finely chopped
- ½ cup olive oil
- ½ cup all-purpose flour
- 2 cups milk
- 2 cups heavy cream
- 2 tsp fresh thyme
- 1 ½ cups Hennessey cognac
- 1 ½ cups fresh or frozen yellow corn, roasted
- 1 ½ cups fresh or frozen white corn, roasted
- 1 bunch fresh chives garnish, finely chopped for garnish
- 2 tbsp fresh ginger, finely chopped
- 2 tbsp fresh garlic, finely chopped
- kosher salt and ground white pepper to taste

Procedure:

In a large 10 qt Dutch oven over medium heat add olive oil then add shallots ginger and garlic cook for 3 minutes then add chicken breast cook for 5 minutes then add your flour stir then cook for 3 minutes add chicken stock to flour and then stir Then add your chicken stock or chicken broth, milk, heavy cream, white and yellow corn, cognac, thyme stir them simmer for 20 minutes then kosher salt and ground white pepper to taste.

Then remove soup from heat then ladle soup into bowls then garnish with finely chopped chives then serve.

"OFF THE HOOK" MANHATTAN CLAM CHOWDER

Makes 5 servings

Ingredients:

3	quarts water
1	pound mussels, frozen shelled
4	10 oz cans baby clams drained, save juice
1 ½	pounds calamari tubes, cut into ¼ rings
1	large onion, small diced
1	medium yellow bell pepper seeded, small diced
1	medium green bell pepper seeded, small diced
3	medium carrots, peeled and diced
1	medium fennel bulb, chopped
2	pounds Yukon gold potatoes, ¼-inch dice
2	pounds plum tomatoes, diced
2	tbsp garlic cloves, chopped
1	tbsp fresh thyme
1	tbsp fresh basil, chopped
2	tbsp fresh parsley, chopped
	Salt and pepper, to taste
	For marinade for seafood
¼	cup Grand Marnier
½	cup Smirnoff orange vodka
½	cup red wine
1	bunch cilantro finely chopped, garnish
1	bunch chives finely chopped, garnish
2	tbsp lemon zest, grated for garnish
2	tbsp orange zest, grated for garnish
2	tbsp lime zest, grated for garnish

Procedure:

First in a large bowl marinate drained clams, mussels, calamari in red wine, orange vodka, grand Marnier 30 minutes to 1 hour then in a large 12 qt Stock pot over medium heat add 3 qts water and reserve clam juice bring it to a simmer then add potatoes, fennel, carrots, onions, garlic, then simmer for 20 minutes then add plum tomatoes, oregano, thyme, basil, peppers, clams, mussels calamari and marinate then simmer for 20 minutes season to taste with salt and pepper then remove chowder from heat then ladle chowder into bowls garnish with fresh cilantro, chives, lemon zest, orange zest, lime zest.

Serve hot in soup bowls

NEW GROOVE FUSION LAMB STEW

Makes 6 servings

Ingredients:

3 ½	pounds lamb shoulder trimmed seasoned floured, cut into 2" cubes
2	pounds Yukon gold potatoes, medium diced
1	pound frozen peas
1	pound frozen lima beans
4	medium carrots peeled, medium diced
5	medium shallots, medium diced
2	cups all-purpose flour seasoned with, salt and pepper
3 ½	cups beef stock or low salt beef broth
¼	cup garlic cloves, chopped
1	tbsp crushed red pepper flakes
3	cups red wine
3	cups brandy
1	cup Smirnoff vodka
½	cup vegetable oil
	Salt and pepper, to taste
¼	cup fresh flat-leaf parsley chopped, for garnish

Procedure:

In a large bowl add 2 cups flour season with salt and pepper then add seasoned lamb meat cubes then toss well in a large 10 qt Dutch oven over medium heal add

Vegetable oil then lamb with ½ cup of the seasoned flour brown on all sides then add potatoes, shallots, beef stock or beef broth then simmer for 45 minutes then

Add crushed red pepper flakes, garlic, peas, lima beans, carrots, red wine, brandy, vodka stir simmer for 25 minutes then season to taste with salt and pepper

Then remove lamb stew from heat then ladle stew into bowls then garnish with chopped parsley serve with crusty bread.

NEW GROOVE CRAB, LOBSTER, OYSTER VEGETABLE SOUP

Makes 5 servings

Ingredients:
- 2 pints shucked oysters, drained
- 1 pound can lobster meat
- 1 pound can jumbo lump crab meat
- 1 bunch carrots, peeled and chopped
- 4 tbsp green onions, slice thin
- 1 tsp crushed red pepper flakes
- 1 16 oz package frozen peas
- 1 16 oz package frozen corn
- 1 quart Whole Milk
- 1 quart heavy cream
- 1 cup Absolut peppar vodka
- 1 cup Bacardi dark rum
- Salt and white pepper, to taste

For roux
- 1 ¼ cups all-purpose flour, add to butter
- 1 ½ sticks sweet butter, melted
- ¼ cup flat leaf parsley chopped, for garnish
- New groove seafood seasoning, to taste
- 2 ½ tbsp fresh garlic, finely chopped
- 2 ½ tbsp fresh ginger, finely chopped

Procedure:

In a 8 qt Dutch oven over medium heat add butter to melt then add flour to make roux stir cook for 4 minutes then lower heat then add carrots, corn, peas, crushed red pepper flakes, garlic and ginger. Milk, Heavy cream, Absolut peppar vodka, Bacardi Dark Rum stir simmer for 14 minutes then add oysters, lobster meat, jumbo lump crab meat, green onions stir simmer for another 15 minutes

Do not boil. Then remove soup from heat then ladle soup into bowls garnish with chopped parsley serve with crackers or crusty bread.

LOBSTER, SHRIMP, TOMATO PASTA SOUP

Makes 6 servings

Ingredients:
- 2 pounds 21/25 shrimp save shells to make stock, shelled and cleaned
- 2 1 pound can lobster meat, chopped
- 3 medium tomatoes, chopped
- 1 bunch green onions, thinly sliced
- ¼ cup fresh parsley, chopped
- 2 cups Burnett vodka
- 1 cup Bacardi dark rum
- 1 cup orecchiette pasta cooked
- 1 tbsp fresh cilantro, chopped
- 1 ½ cups frozen corn
- 1 ½ cups frozen peas
- 4 quarts water
- Salt and pepper, to taste

Procedure:

In a large 10 qt Dutch oven over high heat bring 4 quarts water to a boil. Add shrimp shells then reduce heat cook to medium cook for 15 minutes. Strain shrimp stock then add shrimp stock back to Dutch oven over medium heat. Add pasta and cook for 6 minutes. Add vodka, Dark Rum, tomatoes, peas, corn, green, onions, shrimp lobster meat, parsley, cilantro stir then simmer for 12 minutes. Season to taste with salt and pepper. Then remove soup from heat then pour soup into bowls then serve.

NEW GROOVE GINGER PORK SOUP WITH MANGO

Makes 5 servings

Ingredients:
- 1 pound lean pork tenderloin cleaned, but into strips
- 4 cloves fresh garlic, finely chopped
- 1 4 oz pkg shiitake mushrooms, sliced
- 3 tbsp fresh ginger, finely chopped
- 6 cups beef stock or pork stock
- 1 bunch carrots, peeled and diced
- 1 bunch celery ribs, diced
- 1 medium Vidalia onion, diced
- 2 large ripe mangos peeled sliced grilled, diced
- 5 tbsp peanut oil
- 1 tsp ground allspice
- 1 tsp Chinese 5 spice
- 1 cup jacquin's ginger brandy
- sea salt cracked black pepper to taste
- 1 bunch fresh cilantro chopped, garnish
- 1 bunch fresh Thai basil chopped, garnish

Procedure:

In a large 8 qt Dutch oven over medium heat add peanut oil, garlic, ginger, all-spice, Chinese 5 spice, pork, mushrooms stir cook for 8 minutes then add carrots celery, onions stir. Cook for 6 minutes then add your beef stock or pork stock and ginger brandy. Cook for 10 minutes then add your mango then season to taste with sea salt and cracked black pepper. Remove from heat then pour soup into bowls then garnish with chopped cilantro and chopped Thai basil then serve.

NEW GROOVE FUSION FRUIT SOUP

Makes 5 servings

Ingredients:
- 2 cups fresh peach, whole, med., peeled and sliced
- 2 cups fresh mango, peeled and sliced
- 1 pint fresh strawberries, sliced
- 2 medium bananas, sliced
- 2 ½ cups granulated sugar
- 2 cups water
- ¼ cup Barton peach schnapps
- ¼ cup Kirshwasser cherry brandy
- ¼ cup Champagne
- 3 cups milk
- 3 cups heavy cream
- 1 bunch mint leaves, garnish

Procedure:

First in a large 8 qt Dutch oven combine all fruits, water, sugar, milk, heavy cream, champagne, cherry brandy, and peach schnapps then with a hand blender blend until smooth taste adjust sugar, alcohol then chill then ladle fruit soup into bowls then garnish with fresh mint leaves.

Serve cold in bowls

NEW GROOVE CHICKEN-GINGER CRAWFISH SOUP

Makes 6 servings

Ingredients:
1	1 pound pkg boneless chicken breast, thinly sliced
2	l pound pkg crawfish tail, meat, thawed and drained
3	cups water
3	cups coconut milk
1	small piece ginger, thinly sliced
4	whole garlic cloves, thinly sliced
1	8 oz can straw mushrooms, drained
2	tbsp fish sauce
¼	cup lime juice
1	cup plum tomatoes, medium diced
½	cup yellow tomatoes, medium diced
1	cup penne pasta
¼	cup green onions, thinly sliced
4	tbsp fresh cilantro, chopped
½	cup jacquin's ginger brandy
	Season to taste with Asian-Caribbean Spice Powder

Procedure:

In a large 8 qt Dutch oven over medium high heat add coconut milk and water then bring to a boil then reduce heat to medium then add chicken cook for 4 minutes and then add ginger, garlic, fish sauce, crawfish, mushrooms, pasta, tomatoes, lime juice, ginger brandy, green onions, cilantro stir cook for 15 minutes then season to taste with Asian –Caribbean Spice Powder.

Then remove soup from heat then ladle soup into bowls then serve with crackers.

NEW GROOVE SHRIMP, CHICKEN, CORN TORTILLA SOUP

Makes 10 servings

Ingredients:

8	ears of fresh corn cut off the cob
5	pounds boneless skinless chicken breast medium diced
2	medium red onions, chopped
2	medium jalapeno Chile pepper, seeded and chopped
2	medium Serrano peppers, seeded and chopped
¼	cup garlic cloves, chopped
2	tsp chill powder
¼	cup fresh cilantro, chopped
2	tbsp light brown sugar
1	cup green onions, chopped
2	pounds 16/20 jumbo shrimp, SHELLED AND CLEANED
1	gallon chicken stock or water
1 ¼	cups Jose Cuervo gold tequila
1 ¼	cups Bacardi gold rum ½ cup vegetable oil
1	large bag tortilla chips, garnish
	Season to taste with New Groove Southwest Spice Powder

Procedure:

In a large 10 qt Dutch oven over medium heat add your vegetable oil, then corn, garlic, red onions, jalapeno peppers, Serrano peppers cook for 5 minutes then add chicken stock or water chicken breast, light brown sugar, green onions, cilantro, chill powder, 1 1/4 cups Jose Cuervo gold tequila gold rum then stir then simmer for 20 minutes then add jumbo shrimp stir then simmer for another 6 minutes.

Or till shrimp turns pink season to taste New Groove Southwest Spice Powder then remove soup from heat then ladle soup into bowls then top soup with tortilla chips then serve.

Stocks and Sauces

NEW GROOVE CHICKEN STOCK

Ingredients:

5	quarts water
5	large onions, quartered
5	medium carrots, halved
3	medium celery stalks, halved
2	medium turnips, quartered
2	medium bay leaves
7	cloves garlic
10	small black peppercorns
1	sprig fresh sage leaves
1	sprig fresh rosemary sprigs
1	sprig fresh thyme sprigs
2	pounds chicken breast
1	pound chicken thighs cut into pieces

Procedure:

In a large 12 qt stock pot combine water, vegetables, herbs, chicken thighs, chicken breast heat and bring stock to a boil then reduce heat and bring to a simmer cook for about 1 to2 hours.

And then in a second large stock pot use a double layer of cheesecloth to strain stock into then remove meat, bones, and vegetables keeping liquid skim off any foam or fat from surface.

Let cool and refrigerate.

For soups and sauces.

NEW GROOVE BEEF STOCK

Ingredients:

5	quarts water
5	large onions, quartered
5	medium carrots, halved
3	large celery stalks, halved
2	medium turnips, halved
6	cloves garlic
4	medium bay leaves
10	small black peppercorns
8	fresh sage leaves sprigs
2	fresh rosemary sprigs
2	fresh thyme sprigs
2 ½	pounds beef chuck
2	pounds beef bones
2	cups white wine
4	sprigs fresh parsley

Procedure:

In large 12 qt stock pot combine water, beef bones, beef, vegetables, wine and herbs heat up stock and bring to a boil then reduce to a simmer cook for 3 ½ hours.

Then in a second large stock pot use a double layer of cheesecloth to strain stock into remove meat, bones and vegetables reserve liquid skim off any foam or fat from.

Surface let cool.

For soups, and sauces.

NEW GROOVE VEAL STOCK

Ingredients:

5	quarts water
4	large onions, quartered
5	medium carrots, halved
4	medium celery stalks, halved
3	medium turnips, quartered
3	medium bay leaves
4	small whole cloves
2	sprigs fresh rosemary
2	sprigs fresh thyme
2	cups white wine
10	small black peppercorns
2 ½	pounds veal stew meat
2 ½	pounds veal bones
3	medium veal shanks

Procedure:

In a large 12 quart stock pot combine water, veal stew meat, veal shanks, veal bones, vegetables, white wine, and herbs heat and bring to a boil and reduce stock to a simmer.

And cook for 3 ½ hours then in a second large stock pot use a double layer of cheesecloth to strain stock into them remove meat, bones and vegetables keeping liquid.

Skim off any foam or fat let cool.

For soups, and sauces.

NEW GROOVE FISH STOCK

Ingredients:

- 5 quarts water
- 3 pounds fish bones
- 2 large onions, rough chopped
- 2 large celery stalk, halved
- 3 medium bay leaves
- 9 small black peppercorns
- 1 tsp sea salt
- ½ tsp white pepper
- 1 cup white wine
- 4 sprigs parsley
- 3 sprigs thyme

Procedure:

In a large 8 qt Dutch oven over high heat combine all ingredients bring to a boil then reduce to a simmer cook for 2 hours then in a second saucepot use a double layer of cheesecloth to strain stock into remove all bones, vegetables keeping liquid skim off any foam or fat from surface let cool.

For soups, sauces.

NEW GROOVE SEAFOOD STOCK

Ingredients:
- 5 quarts water
- 3 pounds lobster shells, crab shells, shrimp shells
- 2 large onions, rough chopped
- 2 large celery stalks, rough chopped
- 3 medium bay leaves
- 9 small black peppercorns
- 1 tsp sea salt
- ½ tsp white pepper
- 1 cup white wine
- 3 sprigs thyme

Procedure:

In a large 8 qt Dutch oven over high heat combine all ingredients bring to a boil then reduce to a simmer cook stock for 2 hours then in a second saucepot use a double layer of cheesecloth to strain stock into then remove all shells, and vegetables keeping liquid then skim off any foam or fat from surface let cool.

For soups, and sauces.

NEW GROOVE VEGETABLE STOCK

Ingredients:

5	quarts water
3	large onions, quartered
3	medium carrots, halved
3	medium celery stalks, halved
1 ½	cups turnips, diced small
1 ½	cups leeks, diced small
1 ½	cups potatoes, diced small
1 ½	cups red bell peppers, diced small
2	cups broccoli florets
2	cups corn
2	cups anise, diced small
½	cup basil leaves
½	cup parsley
6	cloves garlic
4	medium bay leaves
2	cups white wine
10	small black peppercorns
½	cup vegetable oil

Procedure:

In a large 8 qt Dutch oven over medium heat add vegetable oil then add vegetables and sauté until golden brown then add water, herbs, wine bring to a boil then reduce to a simmer.

Cook for 2 hours then in a second saucepot strain stock through a double layer of cheesecloth then remove vegetables and keep liquid skim off any foam or fat from surface.

And let cool for soups, sauces.

STOCKS AND SAUCES | 51

NEW GROOVE TURKEY STOCK

Ingredients:

5	quarts water
5	medium onions, quartered
5	medium carrots, halved
4	medium celery stalks, halved
2	medium turnips, quartered
1	medium leek, rough chopped
10	small black peppercorns
3	sprigs parsley
3	sprigs thyme
1	sprig rosemary
1 ½	cups white wine
2	pounds turkey breast meat, cut into pieces
1 ½	pounds turkey thighs cut into pieces

Procedure:

In large 12 qt stock pot combine water, turkey breast meat, turkey thighs, herbs and vegetables bring to a boil and reduce heat to a simmer cook for about 2 hours then in a second stock pot use a double layer of cheesecloth to strain stock into and then remove all meet, bones, vegetables reserve liquid skim off any fat let it sit and cool for soups, and sauces.

NEW GROOVE FUSION VEGETABLE STOCK

Ingredients:

6	quarts of water
3	medium Vidalia onion, quartered
3	medium Bermuda onion, quartered
6	medium carrots, diced
6	medium celery, diced
2	medium turnips, diced
2	medium parsnips, diced
¼	cup fresh garlic, chopped
3 ½	cups fresh yellow sweet corn
1	each red and green bell peppers, seeded and diced
4	medium Yukon gold potato, diced
¼	cup fresh ginger, chopped
5	medium jalapeño peppers, seeded and chopped
5	medium Serrano peppers, seeded and chopped
3 ½	cups fresh wild mushrooms
1	bunch fresh Thai basil
1	small bunch fresh cilantro
1	bunch fresh thyme
1	bunch fresh sage
2	cups Leroux Ginger Brandy
1	cup Hennessy Cognac
1 ½	cups white wine
	Season to taste with new groove house seasoning blend

Procedure:

In a large pot bring water to a simmer then add vegetables and herbs. Simmer 2 hours. In the last 20 minutes add wines, liqueurs and seasonings. Remove from heat and strain. Makes about 2 gallons of stock.

Salads & Greens

My salads scream fusion! All natural fresh ingredients delivered with. An explosion of bright vivid colors,tastes, texures, and aromatics bursting with. Exotic fusion flavors from regions of the Caribbean French-euro continental. And the pacific rim salads can be eaten before or after. Any meal you decide go crazy!

NEW GROOVE
VEGETABLE SAUTE ASPARAGUS

Ingredients:

4	bunches Fresh Asparagus Trimed then blanched
⅓	cup olive oil
2	sticks sweet butter
6	cloves fresh garlic chopped
4	fresh shallots peeled and chopped
1	cup pinenuts
1	cup fresh bread crumbs
½	cup parmesan cheese grated
1	cup champagne
	Kosher salt and coarse ground black pepper to taste

Procedure:

First Trim and blanch your asparagus. Then in a large 8 qt Dutch oven medium high heat add sweet butter, olive oil, garlic, shallots, pinenuts cook for 2 minutes then add your asparagus champagne, stir cook for 4 minutes then stir in bread crumbs, parmesan cheese then season to taste with kosher salt & coarse ground black pepper.

Serves 6 people

SLICK RICK'S ROASTED VEGETABLE JACKPOT OVER ROASTED SPAGHETTI SQUASH

Ingredients:

1 ½	lbs Brussel's sprouts trimmed then cut in half
1	lb small white turnips peeled then medium dice
1	bunch fresh carrot peeled and sliced
4	medium size parsnips peeled and sliced
3 to 4	medium size sweet potatoes peeled medium dice
1	bunch of fresh snow peas strings removed
1 to 2	medium size butternut squash peeled medium dice
1	package of French style green beans
1	pint cherry tomatoes cut in half
1	large yellow bell pepper seeded medium dice
1	medium size head cauliflower cored dice
3	cups wild mushrooms stems remove sliced
1	cup canola oil
	Kosher salt and coarse ground black pepper to taste
1	bunch fresh flat leaf parsley chopped garnish
3 to 4	medium size spaghetti squash cut in half-length wise seeds removed
	Kosher salt to taste
	Ground cinnamon to taste
	Ground nutmeg to taste
	Light brown sugar to taste

Procedure:

First pre-heat your oven at 450°F then take four large baking sheets and then line them with aluminum foil and parchment paper then take two of your large baking sheets place your vegetables on the baking sheets then drizzle canola oil over the vegetables then season with kosher salt and coarse ground black pepper then place your vegetables in the oven roast at 450°F for 25 to 35 minutes or until tender then remove from oven taste vegetables to see if need to be reseasoned then place in a serving dish keep warm.

Then take other two large baking sheet place spaghetti squash cut length wise seeds remove cuts side down roast at 450°F for 45 to 55 minutes or until tender then remove from oven let cool then remove spaghetti squash with a fork to make strands then place in a serving dish season to taste with kosher salt, ground cinnamon ground nutmeg and light brown sugar to serve

Place your spaghetti squash on a dinner plate then top with your roasted vegetables and parsley then serve. Serves 3 to 4 people.

CREAMY HONEY-LIME CITRUS DRESSING

LACED WITH TEQUILA AND RUM

Makes 10 servings

Ingredients:
- 3 cups plain yogurt
- ½ cup honey
- Zest and juice from 1 lime
- Zest and juice from 1 blood orange
- 2 tablespoons fresh ginger, finely chopped
- 2 tablespoons lemon grass, finely chopped
- ¼ cup Jose Cuervo Tequila
- ¼ cup Cruzan Citrus Rum
- 1 medium Habanero Chile pepper, seeded and minced
- 1 medium Anaheim Chile pepper, seeded and minced
- 1 ¼ cups mango chunks with juice

Procedure:

Combine all ingredients into food processor. Blend until smooth and creamy. Transfer to bowl and chill 3 to 4 hours before serving. Serve as a salad dressing or as a marinade for fish and seafood.

NEW GROOVE MEDITERRANEAN SALAD

Makes 5 servings

Ingredients:

- 1   16 oz bag mixed Italian baby greens, cleaned
- 2   medium heads Boston Bibb lettuce, cored and chopped
- 2   yellow tomatoes, small diced
- 2   cups plum tomatoes, small diced
- 2   pounds 21/25 shrimp, cleaned & cooked
- 3   cups bay scallops, cooked
- 1 ½   cups small black olives, pitted
- 1 ½   cups Spanish olives, pitted
- ¼   cup garlic cloves, roasted and chopped for dressing
- 1 ¼   cups Champagne wine vinegar
- 2   cups olive oil
- 2   tbsp fresh oregano, chopped
- 2   tbsp fresh thyme
- 2   tbsp fresh rosemary, chopped
- 2   tbsp fresh basil, chopped
- 1   tsp fresh ginger, chopped
-     Salt and pepper, to taste
-     New Groove Italian-Mediterranean Seasoning (for salad mix)

Procedure:

In a large bowl combine mixed baby greens, Boston Bibb lettuce, yellow tomatoes, plum tomatoes, cooked shrimp, cooked bay scallops, black olives, Spanish olives.

Roasted garlic cloves then toss well. Then in a large bowl add champagne wine vinegar, olive oil, oregano, thyme, rosemary, and basil, ginger then with a hand blender blend until smooth.

Season to taste with salt and pepper the pour over salad greens toss well. Then serve salad on plates.

NEW GROOVE PLANTAIN FRUIT SALAD

Makes 4 servings

Ingredients:
- 4 medium ripe plantains, cooked and sliced
- 4 medium ripe mangos, peeled and sliced
- 2 8 oz cans grapefruit sections, drained
- 2 8 oz cans orange sections, drained
- 1 medium green bell pepper, seeded and sliced
- 2 small red Thai Chile peppers, seeded and sliced
- 2 small cucumbers, diced
- 2 tbsp fresh ginger, finely chopped
- ½ cup shredded coconut, tousled

Recipe for dressing:
- ½ cup canola oil, mix together
- ⅓ cup lime juice, mix together
- ⅓ cup orange juice, mix together
- ½ cup macadamia nut, toasted and crushed
- ⅓ cup Cruzan Banana Rum
- Salt and pepper, to taste

Procedure:

First peel plantains then put plantains in a medium-size saucepan and cover with water then bring to a boil then simmer for 10 minutes or until plantains are tender then drain plantains let cool then slice and then in a large bowl add sliced green pepper, Thai Chile peppers, cucumbers, sliced mangos, grapefruit sections, orange sections, sliced plantains ginger, coconut, macadamia nut.

Medium size bowl add canola oil, lime juice, orange juice Cruzan Banana Rum, then with a hand blender mix until smooth and creamy season to taste with salt and pepper then pour over fruit and vegetables.

Toss well. Then serve fruit salad on salad plates. Garnish with New Groove Caribbean Spice Powder.

Serve at room temp on salad plates.

NEW GROOVE
CAESAR SALAD GONE WILD

Makes 3 servings

Ingredients:
- 3 jumbo eggs
- ¼ cup chicken stock
- 4 small anchovy fillets
- 6 tbsp olive oil
- 2 ½ tbsp lime juice
- 2 tbsp French brandy
- 2 tsp Worcestershire sauce
- 1 ½ tbsp fresh garlic, chopped
- Salt and pepper, to taste
- 1 small head radicchio, cored and julienne
- 1 package chopped romaine, cleaned
- ½ cup parmesan cheese, shavings
- ½ cup Romano cheese, shavings
- 1 package garlic- parmesan croutons, to top salad

Procedure:

In a food processor combine eggs, chicken broth or chicken stock, anchovy filets, olive oil, lime juice, French Brandy, Worcestershire, garlic then pulse for 30 to 60 seconds or until creamy.

And smooth season to taste with salt & pepper remove and pour into a bowl then chill for 3-4 hours then in a large (wooden) bowl add romaine, radicchio, parmesan cheese, Romano cheese.

Then mix in Caesar dressing and toss then serve Caesar salad on plates chilled with garlic-parmesan croutons.

CHEF SIGNATURE RECIPE
NEW GROOVE RHAPSODY SALAD

Makes 4 servings

Ingredients:

1	package mixed salad greens
2	medium plum tomatoes, diced small
1	medium yellow tomato, diced small
1	medium Italian cucumber, medium diced
1	cup kalamata olives, small pitted
1	medium red onion, diced small
½	cup Romano cheese, shavings
1	medium yellow bell pepper cored and cut into, thin rings
1	medium orange bell pepper cored and cut into, thin rings
1	tbsp fresh rosemary, chopped
1	tbsp fresh oregano, chopped
1	10 oz package wild mushrooms, sliced

Rhapsody vinaigrette

½	cup rice wine vinegar
2	tbsp lime juice
1	tbsp lemon zest
1	tbsp fresh rosemary, finely chopped
4	garlic cloves, minced
3	tbsp honey
1	cup ex virgin olive oil

New Groove Italian Mediterranean Seasoning, to taste

Procedure:

In a large mixing bowl combine mixed salad greens, plum tomatoes, yellow tomato, cucumber, olives, red onion, Romano cheese, yellow bell pepper orange bell pepper, oregano, rosemary toss well then chill then for salad dressing mix all ingredients in a food processor blend until smooth.

Then remove dressing from the food processor then drizzle salad dressing over chilled salad then serve salad on plates.

NEW GROOVE CARROT SALAD WITH FIGS AND DATES

Makes 5 servings

Ingredients:

- 2 pounds carrots peeled, cooked and sliced – cut into 3rds
- 1 cup figs, diced
- 1 cup dates, seeded and diced

For dressing

- ½ cup orange juice
- ¼ cup olive oil
- 1 tbsp garlic clove, chopped
- 1 tsp ground cumin
- 1 tsp ground paprika
- ¼ cup fresh parsley, chopped
- Salt and pepper, to taste
- 2 quarts water, see recipe
- 3 tbsp kosher salt, see recipe
- 3 tbsp sweet cream butter
- 3 tbsp extra virgin olive oil

Procedure:

First a large 5 qt Dutch oven over high heat add water, kosher salt bring to a boil then add carrots cook for about ten minutes then rinse under cold water. After carrots have been cooked al dente cool transfers to sauté pan and sauté in butter and olive oil until tender. Remove carrots and add to medium sized bowl along with dates and figs.

Combine orange juice, olive oil, paprika, garlic, cumin, parsley then with a hand blender mix until smooth season to taste with salt and pepper.

Then pour over carrots, figs, dates toss. Then place carrot salad in the refrigerator until ready to serve then serve on salad plates.

NEW GROOVE PASTA SALAD WITH TUNA AND VEGETABLES

Makes 6 servings

Ingredients:
- 1 box tri color penne pasta, cooked and drained
- 5 6 oz yellow fin tuna cooked medium, slice thin
- 1 red onion, slice thin
- 1 bunch asparagus, sliced
- 1 red bell pepper, sliced thin
- 1 yellow bell pepper, sliced thin
- 1 medium zucchini, sliced thin
- 1 yellow squash, sliced thin
- 5 ears of corn cut off the cob, blanched
- 1 12 oz can small pitted black olives, drained

Recipe for dressing
- 2 cups Champagne wine vinegar
- 1 cup olive oil
- ¼ cup fresh chives, finely chopped
- 1 tbsp fresh basil
- 1 tbsp fresh thyme
- 1 tbsp fresh oregano
- Salt and white pepper, to taste

Procedure:

In a large 5 qt mixing bowl combine your cooked pasta, tuna, red onion, asparagus, red bell pepper, yellow bell pepper, zucchini, and yellow squash.

corn, black olives toss well in a medium size bowl add olive oil, champagne wine vinegar, chives, basil, thyme, oregano then with a hand blender blend until.

Smooth then season to taste with salt and white pepper then pour over pasta then toss well then refrigerate pasta salad then serve pasta salad chilled.

On salad plates.

Garnish with New Groove Seafood Seasoning.

CHEF SIGNATURE RECIPE
NEW GROOVE CRAB AND SHRIMP SLAW

Makes 5 servings

Ingredients:
- 1 medium head of cabbage, cored and shredded
- 2 small green bell peppers seeded, slice thin
- 2 small red onions half rings, sliced ¼" thick
- 3 medium Jalapeno Chile peppers seeded, sliced thin
- ¼ cup olive oil
- ½ cup Champagne
- 1 tsp garlic, chopped
- ¼ cup light brown sugar
- ¾ cup mayonnaise
- 1 tsp black sesame seeds
- 1 pinch cayenne pepper
- 1 dash Tabasco sauce
- Salt and white pepper, to taste
- 1 pound jumbo 16/20 shrimp, cleaned & cooked
- 1 pound jumbo lump crab meat, drained

Procedure:

In a large bowl combine shredded cabbage, sliced green peppers, jalapeno pepper, red onion, jumbo shrimp, jumbo lump crab meat black sesame seeds, and mayo then mix well and then in a medium size bowl combine olive oil, champagne, garlic, light brown sugar dash Tabasco sauce, pinch of cayenne pepper blend well.

Salt and white pepper to taste then pour over slaw toss well then put in fridge chill for 3 hours until ready to serve then serve chilled on plates.

Serve with crackers on plates or with BBQ Chicken or BBQ Ribs.

NEW GROOVE CRAB, SCALLOP TOMATO SEAFOOD SALAD

Makes 5 servings

Ingredients:
- 2 pound jumbo lump crab meat, seeded
- 2 cups medium size bay scallops see recipe
- 2 pound 21/25 shrimp, cleaned butter flied
- 5 medium plum tomatoes, medium diced
- 3 medium yellow tomatoes, medium diced
- 1 cup red onion, small diced
- 2 tbsp garlic cloves, finely chopped
- 2 tbsp fresh ginger, finely chopped
- 2 tbsp fresh shallots, finely chopped
- 2 cups black olives, small pitted
- 1 cup pecans, chopped and toasted
- ½ cup black raisins
- ½ cup golden raisins
- 2 tbsp fresh thyme
- 2 tbsp fresh oregano, chopped

For dressing
- ¼ cup Jose Cuervo tequila
- ¼ cup Champagne
- 1 cup honey
- ⅓ cup Canola oil
- ½ cup olive oil
- Salt and pepper, to taste
- ⅓ cup vegetable oil
- 1 16 oz bag mixed field greens, see recipe, cleaned

Procedure:

First in a large 8 qt Dutch oven over medium heat add vegetable oil, garlic, ginger, shallots, thyme, oregano, bay scallops, shrimp stir cook for 5 minutes then remove from heat let cool then in a large bowl combine tomatoes, red onions, black olives, pecans, golden raisins, black raisins, jumbo lump crab meat, shrimp, bay scallops then toss well and then in a large bowl.

Combine olive oil, canola oil, champagne, tequila, honey then with a hand blender mix until smooth season to taste with salt and pepper then pour on tomato seafood salad toss well.

Serve on mixed field greens on salad plates.

NEW GROOVE SALAD WITH VINAIGRETTE DRESSING

Makes 5 servings

Ingredients:
- 1   16 oz bag mixed salad greens, cleaned
- 1   small head Boston lettuce, washed and dried
- 1   small head romaine lettuce, washed and dried
- 1   small head curly top lettuce, washed and dried

   For vinaigrette dressing
- 1 ½   cups olive oil
- ⅔   cup Champagne wine vinegar
- ¼   cup lime juice
- ¼   cup fresh garlic, finely chopped
- ¼   cup Jose Cuervo tequila
- 3   tbsp dry mustard
- 2   tbsp fresh parsley, finely chopped

   Salt and white pepper, to taste

Procedure:

In a large bowl combine all greens mix well then in another large bowl add olive oil, champagne wine vinegar, lime juice, garlic, tequila, dry mustard, chopped parsley then with a hand blender.

Mix until smooth season to taste salt and white pepper then pour dressing over salad greens toss well then serve on salad plates.

NEW GROOVE ROASTED EGGPLANT AND PEPPER SALAD

Makes 5 servings

Ingredients:

- 5 medium plum tomatoes, medium diced
- 1 medium yellow tomato, medium diced
- 1 medium red bell pepper, julienne
- 1 medium yellow bell pepper, julienne
- 1 medium orange bell pepper, julienne
- 1 medium green bell pepper, julienne
- 1 medium red onion cut in half, julienne
- 4 tbsp red wine vinegar
- 2 tbsp garlic cloves, finely chopped
- 1 12 oz package baby spinach
- 1 12 oz package mixed salad greens
- 5 tbsp olive oil
- 2 tsp dried basil
- 2 tsp dried rosemary
- 4 medium eggplants medium diced, roasted
- Salt and pepper, to taste

Procedure:

In a large bowl combine eggplant and sweet bell peppers and 2 tablespoons of olive oil, 1/2 tablespoon of garlic, basil, and rosemary and toss well

Then add 2 tablespoons of red wine vinegar and salt and pepper to taste then transfer to a foil- lined sheet pan and spread evenly on pan meanwhile preheat oven to 425°F and bake for 25 minutes or until tender then remove from oven then chill then in another large bowl combine yellow tomato, plum tomatoes.

Red onion, garlic, baby spinach, mixed salad greens, olive oil, basil, rosemary toss well season to taste with salt and pepper then place salad greens on salad plates.

Then top with roasted eggplant and roasted peppers then serve.

NEW GROOVE PASTA SALAD

Makes 5 servings

Ingredients:

1	1 pound box bow tie pasta, cooked cooled
1	small bunch scallions, finely chopped
2	cups garbanzo beans, canned, rinsed and drained
2	cups pitted black olives, drained
1 ½	cups pitted green olives, drained
1	medium red bell pepper seeded, medium diced
1	medium yellow bell pepper seeded, medium diced
1	medium orange bell pepper seeded, medium diced
2	medium Red Thai chille peppers, seeded and minced
1 ½	cups yellow corn, frozen, roasted
1 ½	cups white corn kernels, frozen, roasted
1 ½	cups broccoli florets, small
1 ½	cups carrots peeled, small diced
3	cups Genoa salami cut 1/4 inch thick, medium diced

Recipe for dressing

1	cup olive oil
2	tbsp fresh ginger, peeled and minced
½	cup red wine vinegar
2	tbsp lemon juice
1 ½	tbsp garlic, finely chopped
1 ½	tbsp fresh dill, chopped
2	tbsp fresh parsley, chopped
2	tbsp honey
	Salt and pepper, to taste

Procedure:

Combine all salad ingredients together in a large bowl and toss then in a food processor combine all dressing ingredients together and pulse for 60 to 90 seconds or until smooth season to taste with salt and pepper.

Then pour over salad toss well then serve pasta salad on salad plates.

NEW GROOVE
FRENCH STYLE GREEN BEANS

Makes 5 servings

Ingredients:
- 2 pounds fresh green beans, cleaned
- ½ cup olive oil
- ¼ cup fresh garlic cloves, chopped
- ½ cup fresh bread crumbs
- 1 cup chopped pecans
- 1 cup chopped hazelnuts
- ½ cup champagne
- Salt and pepper to taste
- 3 cup water for green beans

Procedure:

First in a large 8 qt Dutch oven over high heat add water bring to a boil add green beans cook for 3 minutes then drain the green beans then run under cold water to stop cooking process and then in the same Dutch oven over medium heat add your olive oil then green beans, champagne, garlic, hazelnuts, pecans, bread crumbs cook for 4 minutes season to taste with salt and pepper.

Vegetable side dish.

NEW GROOVE FUSION BAKED ACORN SQUASH

Makes 5 servings

Ingredients:

- 5 medium acorn squash, cleaned and quartered
- 1 stick sweet butter
- ¼ cup Hennessy cognac
- ¼ cup Bacardi dark rum
- ¼ cup French apple brandy calvados
- 1 cup light brown sugar
- 1 cup maple syrup
- 1 tsp ground cinnamon
- ½ tsp ground nutmeg

Procedure:

First preheat oven at 450°F then in a medium size saucepan over medium heat combine butter, light brown sugar, maple syrup, dark rum, cognac, French apple brandy, cinnamon, nutmeg then stir then bring mixture to a simmer then place acorn squash in a 10 by baking dish then pour mixture over acorn squash then bake at 450°F for 30 to 35 minutes or until soft.

Vegetable or side dish.

NEW GROOVE BROCCOLI RABE WITH BLACK WALNUTS AND CHAMPAGNE

Makes 5 servings

Ingredients:

2	pounds broccoli Rabe, trimmed
1	cup olive oil
⅓	cup fresh garlic cloves, chopped
1	tbsp crushed red pepper
½	cup fresh bread crumbs
1	black walnuts, toasted
1	cup Champagne
	Salt and pepper, to taste
2 ½	quarts water for broccoli Rabe, coocked and drained
3	tbsp kosher salt, add to water

Procedure:

In a large 5 qt Dutch oven over high head add water kosher salt bring to a boil then add broccoli Rabe to cook for 2 minutes then transfer to a large bowl of ice water.

Then drain and squeeze out water then in a large 5 qt Dutch oven over medium heat add olive oil, red pepper flakes, black walnuts, garlic, broccoli Rabe, and Champagne.

Bread crumbs stir cook for 5 minutes season to taste with salt and pepper serve hot!

Vegetable dish or side dish and over pasta.

NEW GROOVE FUSION GLAZED BABY CARROTS

Makes 5 servings

Ingredients:
- 2 packages baby carrots
- 1 stick sweet butter
- ½ cup light brown sugar
- 1 cup maple syrup
- ¼ cup Bacardi dark rum
- ¼ cup fresh parsley, chopped
- ¼ cup laird's apple jack brandy
- 2 cups water
- Salt and pepper to taste

Procedure:

First in a large 5 qt Dutch oven over medium heat add water bring to a boil add carrots cook for 3 minutes then drain then put aside then in a medium size saucepan over medium heat add your butter, brown sugar, maple syrup, dark rum, apple jack brandy stir bring to a simmer for 3 minutes and then pour the glaze over carrots in the Dutch oven.

Then place Dutch oven over medium heat simmer for 3 minutes then add your parsley season to taste with salt and pepper.

Vegetable side dish.

NEW GROOVE MUSTARD GREENS WITH CABBAGE 'TAKE' 1

Makes 6 servings

Ingredients:
- ½ pound smoked turkey breasts, cut into ¼" pieces
- 4 bunches mustard greens stems removed, washed and sliced
- 1 medium cabbage head, cored and sliced
- 2 medium Italian hot peppers, seeded and sliced
- 1 medium Vidalia onion, chopped
- ¼ cup fresh marjoram, chopped
- ¼ cup granulated sugar
- 1 cup champagne
- 2 cups water
- Salt and pepper, to taste

Procedure:

In a large 8 qt oven over medium heat add smoked turkey breast cook for 2 minutes then add the mustard greens, cabbage cover and lower the heat cook for 10 minutes then uncover then add water, onions, hot peppers champagne, marjoram sugar stir cover and cook over low heat for 1 hour or until greens and cabbage are tender then season to taste with salt and pepper.

Vegetable side dish.

NEW GROOVE OKRA, CORN, TOMATOES WITH PEPPERS, ONIONS

Makes 4 servings

Ingredients:
- 1 ½   pounds fresh okra, cut ½ inch thick
- 3   medium plum tomatoes, diced
- 3   medium ears of corn cut off the cob
- 2   medium Vidalia onions, sliced
- 3   medium jalapeno peppers, seeded and sliced
- ½   cup pine nuts
- ½   cup vegetable oil
-         Salt and pepper to taste

Procedure:

In a large 5 qt Dutch oven over medium heat add oil then corn, hot peppers, onions, okra, pine nuts plum tomatoes stir cook for 6 minutes then season to taste with salt and pepper.

Vegetables side dish.

NEW GROOVE GREEN BEANS

Makes 5 servings

Ingredients:

½	cup olive oil
2	medium Serrano peppers, seeded and chopped
½	cup fresh bread crumbs
1 ½	pounds fresh green beans, blanched
2	tbsp fresh ginger, chopped
2	tbsp fresh garlic cloves, chopped
3	medium plum tomatoes, diced
3	medium ears of corn cut off the cob
⅓	cup Champagne
	Salt and pepper, to taste

Procedure:

First blanch the green beans then shock in cold water to stop cooking then in a large 8 qt Dutch oven over medium heat add olive oil, garlic, ginger, corn, chili peppers then cook for 3 minutes then add green beans, plum tomatoes, bread crumbs champagne stir cook for 6 minutes season to taste with salt and pepper.

Vegetable side dish.

NEW GROOVE RATATOUILLE SAUTE

Ingredients:
- 2   medium size red onions peeled diced
- 1   medium size orange bell pepper seeded diced
- 1   medium size yellow bell pepper seeded diced
- 1   medium size red bell pepper seeded diced
- 1   medium size green bell pepper seeded diced
- 2   medium size Italian eggplant peeled diced
- 2   medium size Zucchini diced
- 5   medium size Plum tomatoes diced
- 6   cloves fresh garlic chopped
- ⅓   cup olive oil
- ½   cup pinenuts
- ⅓   cup Gosling's black seal Rum
- ⅓   cup Champagne
- 1   small bunch fresh flat'leaf parsley chopped
-     Kosher salt & coarse ground black pepper to taste

Procedue:

First in a large 8 qt Dutch oven over medium high heat add olive oil, then garlic, pinenuts red onions stir cook for 3 minutes then add all your bell peppers, black rum, champagne eggplant zucchini, plum tomatoes stir cook for 8 minutes then stir in parsley then season to taste with kosher salt & coarse ground black pepper

Serves 4 people

Rice & Pasta
Other Starches

Invented by the Chinese embraced loved and kicked up by Italian cultures pasta. Is always a favorite at the dinner table and with the of pasta on the market today. The possibilities are endless on what you can cook up to me. Pasta by itself is a lonely suit waiting to be all dressed up. And a night out on the town. I dress up my pasta dishes with a wide variety of sauces from tomato based to cream. I go crazy tossing in fresh vegetables, herbs, spices and all sorts of flavorings which makes for a slammin lunch or dinner. And don't forget my pastas are unique because I also throw them a few twist/ and curves then serve them up hot and fresh and bursting with fusion flavors.

NEW GROOVE CHICKEN N PASTA TWISTED

Ingredients:

- 7 boneless chicken breast cleaned seasoned with Kosher salt and coarse ground black pepper pan seared then sliced
- 1 lb package penne pasta cooked
- 6 cloves garlic chopped
- 6 fresh shallots peeled chopped
- 3 leeks cleaned and sliced thin
- 9 Plum tomatoes diced
- ⅓ cup olive oil
- 1 cup pinenuts toasted
- 2 Tablespoons fresh basil chopped
- 2 Tablespoons fresh oregano chopped
- 2 Tablespoons fresh Margoram chopped
- 2 Tablespoons fresh thyme
- 2 Tablespoons fresh flat leaf parsley chopped
- 1 Tablespoon crushed red pepper flakes
- 1 cup Absolut Pepper Vodka
- 2 cups Champagne

Kosher salt and coarse ground black pepper to taste.

Procedure:

First in a large 8 qt Dutch oven over medium high heat add olive oil then seasoned chicken breast 4 minutes per side then remove chicken breast put aside then slice chicken then add shallots garlic crushed red pepper flakes, lecks Tomatoes, Pinenuts champagne, pepper codka.

Stir cook for 5 minutes, then add your sliced chicken, oregano, basil, parsley, thyme marjoram stir cook for another 5 minutes season to taste Kosher salt and coarse ground black pepper. Then on a large serving platter add your cooked penne pasta then spoon chicken mixture over pasta Garnish with grated parmesan.

Cheese serves 5

NEW GROOVE PASTA WITH LOBSTER AND CHICKEN

Ingredients:

- 1 lb box Fettuccine pasta cooked
- 2 gallons water ¼ cup olive oil ¼ cup kosher salt
- ⅓ cup olive oil for cooking chicken
- 3 cloves fresh garlic chopped
- 3 fresh shallots peeled chopped
- 2 Tablespoons fresh flat leaf parsley chopped
- 2 Tablespoons fresh Thyme
- 2 Tablespoons fresh Oregano chopped
- 1 cup walnuts toasted
- 1 cup pinenuts toasted
- 4 boneless chicken breast season with kosher salt & coarse ground black pepper
- 2 1lb Lobster meat
- ⅓ cup Absolut pepper vodka
- ⅓ cup Hennessy black cognac
- 3½ cups Heavy cream
- 2 cups crumbled Gorgonzola cheese
-   Kosher salt & Coarse ground black pepper

Procedure:

First pre heat oven at 375° then place nuts on a baking sheet toast them for 10 minutes then remove from oven. Put aside. In a large 5 quart dutch oven over high heat it should say. Cook pasta al-dente then drain toss with cold water to stop cooking then place pasta in bowl toss pasta with a small amount of oil to keep from sticking then in a large 3 quart saute pan over medium high heat add olive oil then your seasoned chicken breast pan sear chicken breast 3 minutes per side then remove pan from heat then slice your chicken breast then return pan over medium heat then add garlic, shallots Toasted nuts saute for 2 minutes then add your sliced chicken, lobster meat, pepper vodka, black cognac it should say season with kosher salt and coarse ground black pepper then spoon sauce over pasta toss the top with gorgonzola cheese. Serves 4 people.

NEW GROOVE RISOTTO TWISTED

Ingredients:

- 5 fresh shallots peeled and chopped
- 6 cloves fresh garlic chopped
- 2 carrots peeled and chopped
- 2 celery stalks chopped
- 2 Italian peppers seeded and chopped
- 1 cup sliced wild mushrooms
- 1 cup pinenuts toasted
- 2 cups risotto rice
- 1 cup grated parmesan cheese
- 4 cups hot chicken stock
- 1 ½ cups champagne
- 1 cup Gosling's Black Seal Rum
- ⅔ cup olive oil
- 2 Tablespoons fresh thyme
- 2 Tablespoons fresh oregano chopped
- 2 Tablespoons fresh flat leaf parsley chopped
- 2 Tablespoons fresh basil chopped
- Kosher salt and coarse ground black pepper to taste

Procedure:

In a large 8 qt Dutch oven over medium heat add olive oil, shallots, garlic carrots celery, peppers wild mushrooms, champagne, rum rice stir until rice is coated with oil about 3 minutes then add your hot chicken stock one ladel at a time stir until all your stock absorbed about 12 minutes then stir in parmesan cheese, thyme basil oregano then season to taste with kosher salt and coarse ground black pepper.

Serves 7

NEW GROOVE ROASTED YUKON GOLD POTATOES

Ingredients:

4	lbs Yukon Gold Potatoes ½ inch diced
7	cloves fresh garlic chopped
5	Shallots peeled chopped
2	medium Italian peppers seeded medium diced
½	cup pinenuts
1	cup olive oil
2	Tablespoons fresh Rosemary leaves chopped
2	Tablespoons fresh flat leaf parsley chopped
2	Tablespoons fresh oregano chopped
2	Tablespoons fresh Thyme
2	Tablespoons fresh marjoram chopped
2½	Tablespoons Paprika

Kosher Salt & coarse ground black pepper to taste!

Procedure:

First Pre-heat oven at 350°F. Then in a large mixing bowl add diced potatoes, pepper, garlic, shallots, paprika, pinenuts, thyme, parsley, oregano, majaram, rosemary. Toss well then transfer to baking sheets. Roast potatoes at 350°F for 45 minutes to 1 hour or until tender. Season to taste with Kosher salt coarse black pepper. Serves 6 people.

NEW GROOVE SEAFOOD BOLOGNESE

Ingredients:
- 2 lbs Fresh Chili Pasta cooked
- 2 lbs cuttlefish sliced
- 2 lbs cans Lobster meat
- 2 lbs Fresh monkfish diced
- 6 Fresh shallots peeled diced roasted
- 4 Fresh carrots peeled diced roasted
- 4 Fresh celery ribs diced roasted
- 4 Fresh parsnips peeled diced roasted
- 4 lbs ground meatloaf mix
- 1 cup pinenuts roasted
- ⅓ cup tomato paste
- 1 ⅓ cups beef stock
- 1 ⅓ cups merlot wine
- ⅓ Fresh flat leaf parsley chopped
- Kosher salt & coarse ground black pepper to taste.
- 1 cup olive oil to brown meat

Procedure:

First pre heat oven to 350°F Then place on a large baking sheet diced shallots, carrots celery parsnips, Pinenuts roast for 15 minutes then remove from oven. Put aside then in a large 8 quart Dutch oven over medium heat add olive oil then meatloaf mix brown meat on all sides breakup meat drain off the fat then return meat back to Dutch oven. Then add roasted vegetables over. Pinenuts sliced cuttlefish, monkfish lobster meat tomato paste, beef stock merlot wine. Stir simmer for 1 hour then stir in sour cream Parsley season to taste with kosher salt and coarse ground black pepper. Serve with chili pasta. Serves 8 people.

NEW GROOVE SEAFOOD SAUTE OVER SAFFRON PASTA

Ingredients:
- 5   Shallots peeled, diced
- 7   cloves fresh garlic chopped
- ¼   lb Pancetta bacon sliced thin then diced
- ⅓   cup olive oil
- ⅓   cup pinenuts
- 1   small bunch fresh oregano chopped
- 1   small bunch fresh thyme
- 1   small bunch fresh basil chopped
- 2   cups champagne
- 1   cup Jose Cuervo Gold Tequilla
- 10 medium size plum tomatoes chopped
- 1   lb 16/20 Jumbo shrimp shelled n cleaned
- 1   lb can Jumbo lump crab meat
- 1   lb Bay scallops
- 1   lb package crawfish tail meat
- 1   lb can lobster meat
- 1   lb fresh saffron pasta cooked
-     Kosher salt & coarse ground black pepper to taste

Procedure:

First in a large 8 quart dutch oven over medium heat add olive oil pinenuts shallots, pancetta bacon, garlic stir cook for 4 minutes add plum tomatoes shrimp bay scallops crawfish crab meat, tequila, champagne stir cook for 10 minutes then stir in basil thyme, oregano season to taste with kosher salt & coarse ground black pepper toss with saffron pasta.

Serves 6 people.

CHEF RICK'S NEW GROOVE ORZO MEDLEY

Makes 8 servings

Ingredients:
- 2 cups uncooked orzo pasta in chicken broth, cooked
- 3 cups plum tomatoes, small diced
- 1 cup yellow corn, roasted
- 1 cup white corn, roasted
- 6 medium garlic cloves roasted, slice thin
- 1 cup kalamata olives, small pitted
- 1 small head radicchio, cored and julienne
- 1 ⅔ cups pine nuts, toasted
- 3 Thai red chilies peppers, seeded and diced

Recipe for dressing
- 1 cup olive oil
- ½ cup Champagne wine vinegar
- ¼ cup kalamata olive save, juice from olives
- ⅓ cup honey
- 1 tsp garlic, chopped
- Salt and pepper, to taste
- 1 ½ quarts chicken stock to cook orzo

Procedure:

In a large bowl combine plum tomatoes, yellow and white corn, garlic, kalamata olives, radicchio, pine nuts and chili peppers then blend well meanwhile in a 4 qt saucepan.

Cook orzo in chicken stock until tender drain and add to salad when chilled then toss salad until well blended for the salad dressing blend all ingredients in food processor.

Add ½ cup to salad mixture then serve.

Serve chilled on plates.

NEW GROOVE BUTTERMILK, GARLIC, CHEESE MASHED POTATOES 'TAKE' 1

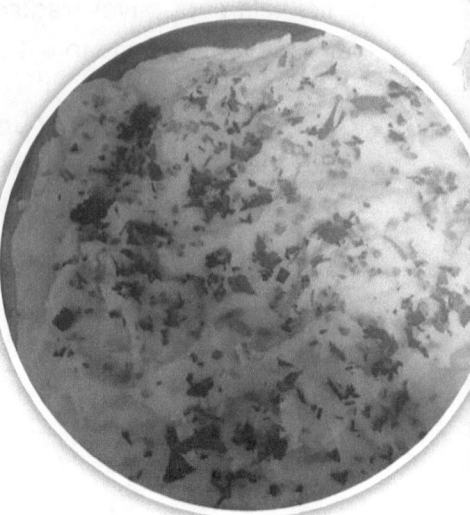

Makes 5 servings

Ingredients:
- 3 ½ pounds Yukon gold potatoes
- 1 ¼ cups buttermilk
- 1 cup boursin cheese
- ½ cup garlic cloves, roasted
- 2 sticks sweet butter, softened
- 2 quarts water, for potatoes
- Salt and white pepper, to taste
- 2 tablespoons flat leaf parsley chopped, garnish

Procedure:

In a large 8 qt Dutch oven over medium heat add water, Yukon gold potatoes then bring to a simmer cook potatoes for 25 minutes or until fork tender.

Then drain the potatoes then add potatoes back to Dutch oven then add your butter, boursin cheese, garlic, and buttermilk then with a hand blender mix until.

Smooth season to taste with salt and white pepper. Then put mashed in a serving dish then garnish with chopped parsley then serve.

Good with roasted chicken veal pork and beef.

Side dish

NEW GROOVE FUSION WILD RICE 'TAKE' 1

Makes 6 servings

Ingredients:
- 1 package wild rice
- 2 cups white rice
- 4 cups chicken stock or water
- 1 cup pecans, chopped
- 1 cup dates, chopped
- 1 cup dried cranberries
- 1 cup Hennessey cognac
- Salt and pepper, to taste

Procedure:

In a large 4 qt saucepot over high heat add chicken stock or water bring to a boil add wild rice then reduce heat to medium cook for an hour in the last 20 minutes of cooking wild rice

Add the cognac, white rice, pecans, dates, cranberries stir cook for the final 20 minutes let rice stand for 5 minutes off the heat then season to taste with salt and pepper then put.

Then put wild rice in a serving dish then serve.

Side dish

NEW GROOVE WILD MUSHROOM AND WILD RICE

Makes 6 servings

Ingredients:

- 2 pounds fresh wild mushrooms see recipe
- 4 tbsp olive oil
- ½ cup carrots peeled, finely chopped
- ½ cup red onions peeled, finely chopped
- ½ cup celery, finely chopped
- ½ cup fennel, finely chopped
- 2 ½ tablespoons garlic cloves, finely chopped
- 2 tablespoons fresh ginger minced
- 3 Red Thai Chile peppers, seeded and minced
- 2 tbsp fresh cilantro, chopped
- 2 ¼ cups wild rice
- 7 ½ cups vegetable stock
- Salt and pepper, to taste

Procedure:

Take one pound of the wild mushrooms and finely chop them then take the remaining one pound wild mushrooms and slice them in half.

Then in a large 5 qt Dutch oven over medium heat add olive oil, and then carrots, red onions, celery, fennel stir cook for 10 minutes then add ginger, garlic, Thai Chile peppers stir cook for 3-4 minutes then stir in your finely chop wild mushrooms, vegetable stock, wild rice then bring to a boil then reduce to simmer cook for 50 minutes then add the remaining sliced wild mushrooms, cilantro stir and cook for another 10 minutes remove from heat season to taste with salt and pepper then put rice in a serving dish then serve rice.

Side dish

CHEF GANT'S "GROOVIN" RICE PILAF

Makes 6 servings

Ingredients:
- 2 cups white rice
- 4 cups water
- 3 tbsp sweet butter
- 1 cup red onion, chopped
- 1 cup celery, chopped
- 1 cup carrots, chopped
- 1 cup pine nuts, toasted
- 1 cup hazelnuts, chopped and toasted
- ½ cup Bacardi gold rum
- Salt, to taste
- 2 tablespoons flat leaf parsley chopped, garnish

Procedure:

In a large 8 qt Dutch oven over high heat add water then bring to a boil then add your butter, rice, onion, carrots, celery, rum, hazelnuts, pine nuts stir then reduce heat bring to a simmer cook for 20 minutes then turn off heat and let rice pilaf stand for 5 minutes stir season to taste with salt. Then put Rice pilaf in a serving dish then garnish with chopped parsley then serve. Good with fish, veal, pork, chicken, beef

Side dish

CHEF GANT'S NEW GROOVE STUFFED TWICE BAKED POTATOES

Ingredients:

- 4 lbs. Russet Potatoes, Baked, see recipe
- 1 ½ Stick Sweet Butter
- 1 ½ cups Milk
- 1 cup fresh flatleaf parsley chopped
- 1 cup fresh chives chopped
- 1 cup extra sharp cheddar cheese, see recipe
- 1 cup bacon cooked and crumbled
- 1 cup Italian sweet sausage casing removed, cooked and crumbled
- 1 cup Italian hot sausage casing removed, cooked, and crumbled

  kosher salt and ground white pepper to taste.

Procedure:

First preheat oven at 450°f then on a large baking sheet russet potatoes then bake for 40 minutes then remove potatoes length wise in half then scoop out middle leaving a border then in a large pot over medium heat add sweet butter, milk cook for 3 minutes then remove from heat add the scoop-out potato back into potato shells. Top with hot sausage, sweet sausage, bacon, parsley, chives, cheese then place stuffed potatoes on a large baking sheet bake at 450 f for 8 to 10 minutes or until cheese melts then remove potatoes from oven then place stuffed potatoes on a serving platter then serve.

CHEF RICK'S PERFECT PASTA
WITH SEAFOOD AND TOMATOES

Makes 8 servings

Ingredients:
- 2 pounds fresh extra large shrimp, shelled and cleaned
- 1 pound fresh baby bay scallops, cleaned
- 2 1 pound cans lobster meat, cleaned
- 1 pound little neck clams, cleaned
- 1 bunch Thai basil, for garnish
- 2 16 oz cans crushed tomatoes in juice'
- ½ cup cilantro, finely chopped
- 6 fresh garlic cloves, finely chopped
- 1 large red onion, finely chopped
- 3 1/2 cups Bacardi gold rum
- 2 1/2 cups French brandy
- 1 cup champagne
- ½ cup olive oil
- 1 box bow tie pasta, cooked and drained
- Salt and pepper, to taste
- Parmesan cheese, grated for garnish
- Romano cheese, granted for garnish
- 1 cup pine nuts, toasted for garnish
- 2 quarts water

Procedure:

In a large sauce pot over medium heat, heat oil. Add garlic and onions. Sauté for 5 minutes and season with salt and pepper. Add crushed tomatoes, Thai basil, cilantro, ½ gold rum, 1 cup champagne and 1cup brandy. Cover and cook for 35 to 40 minutes on medium low heat. Meanwhile, in another large sauce pot, add 2 qts of water, 2 cups of gold rum and 1 ½ cups of brandy. Bring to boil add seafood. Cook until seafood is no longer opaque. Remove from heat and reserve water. Transfer seafood to tomato sauce and mix in. Cover and cook for 5 to 7 minutes. Cook pasta in reserve water until al dente. Toss pasta, seafood and tomato sauce together. Grate fresh parmesan and Romano cheeses over top. Garnish with sprigs of Thai basil and toasted pine nuts. Serve with a green salad.

PASTA WITH SHRIMP, SAUSAGE AND SHITAKI MUSHROOMS

Makes 6 servings

Ingredients:
- 1   16 oz box tri colored bowtie pasta, cooked
- 1 ½ lbs 16/20 shrimp peeled, cleaned and butter flied
- 2 ½ lbs sweet Italian sausage casing removed, crumbled
- 2   cups shiitake mushrooms stems removed, julienne
- 1 ½ tablespoons fresh garlic, finely chopped
- 1   tablespoon fresh ginger, finely chopped
- 2   medium Italian hot peppers, seeded and diced
- 1   medium white onion, diced
- ½   cup pine nuts, lightly toasted
- 6   medium roma tomato, diced small
- 3 ½ tablespoons olive oil
- 2   tablespoons sweet cream butter
- 3   cups chicken stock, see recipe
- 1 ½ cups white wine
- 1 ½ cups Hennessy Cognac
- 1   tablespoon fresh basil, finely chopped
- 1   tablespoon fresh sage, finely chopped
- 1   tablespoon fresh thyme, finely chopped
-      Salt and white pepper, to taste

Procedure:

In a large sauté pan over medium heat add sausage. Stir and sauté for about 10 minutes or until sausage is browned. Remove sausage and drain any excess fat. Return to the stove and heat olive and butter. Add garlic and ginger. Stir and sauté for 4 minutes then add onions, pine nuts, hot peppers and mushrooms. Stir and sauté for 6 to 7 minutes then add sausage, shrimp, tomatoes, stock, wine, cognac and herbs. Reduce heat to low and cover. Simmer 10 to 12 minutes then add pasta. Toss or stir with spoon until pasta is well coated. Season to taste with salt and white pepper.

Serve hot. Garnish with fresh chopped basil and sage. Sprinkle with diced hot Italian peppers. Finish with grated parmesan or Romano cheese.

ORZO WITH CHILI'S, ONIONS, PEAS AND PROSCIUTTO

Makes 6 servings

Ingredients:

2 ½	cups orzo pasta, cooked in chicken stock until tender
4	medium Jalapeño Chile pepper, seeded and diced
4	medium Anaheim Chile pepper, seeded and diced
1	medium Vidalia onion, diced small
1 ½	tablespoons fresh garlic, finely chopped
1 ½	tablespoons fresh ginger, finely chopped
2	cups frozen peas, thawed
⅓	lb prosciutto sliced thin, diced ¼"
½	cup pine nuts, lightly toasted
½	cup kalamata olives pitted, finely chopped
1	tablespoon fresh basil, finely chopped
1	tablespoon fresh sage, finely chopped
1	tablespoon fresh thyme, finely chopped
3 ½	tablespoons olive oil
3	tablespoons sweet cream butter
2 ½	cups chicken stock
1 ½	cups white wine
	Season to taste with "Salt and white pepper"

Procedure:

In a large sauté pan over medium heat, heat olive oil and butter. Add garlic and ginger and stir and sauté for 4 minutes. Add prosciutto and stir and sauté for 4 to 5 minutes. Add onions, peppers, peas, pine nuts and olives. Stir and sauté for 5 to 6 minutes then add chicken stock, wine and herbs. Season with salt and white pepper. Reduce heat to low and cover. Simmer about 6-8 minutes or until most of liquid has been absorbed. Add pasta and toss or stir with spoon until pasta is coated. Remove from heat and serve with fresh grated parmesan cheese and some toasted pine nuts.

PASTA WITH LOBSTER, CRAB, SHRIMP, SAUSAGE AND MUSHROOMS

Makes 6 servings

Ingredients:

1	16 oz box tricolor bowtie pasta, cooked and drained
1	1 lb can lobster meat
1	1 lb can jumbo lump crab meat
1	2 lb bag 16/20 jumbo shrimp cleaned shelled, butter flied
2	lbs sweet Italian sausage casing removed, crumbled
2	cups fresh shiitake mushrooms stems removed, julienne
2	tablespoons fresh garlic cloves, finely chopped
2	tablespoons fresh ginger, finely chopped
2	medium Italian hot peppers, seeded and diced
1	medium white onion peeled, medium diced
½	cup pine nuts, lightly toasted
6	medium Roma tomatoes, diced small
4	tablespoons olive oil
2	tablespoons sweet butter
1 ⅓	cups chicken stock
½	cup white wine
½	cup Hennessey cognac
1	tablespoon fresh basil, finely chopped
1	tablespoon fresh sage, finely chopped
1	tablespoon fresh thyme leaves
	Kosher salt and white pepper, to taste
2	cups parmesan cheese shavings, for garnish

Procedure:

In a large 8 qt Dutch oven over medium heat add Italian sweet sausage then stir and cook for 10 minutes or until sausage is browned then remove sausage from Dutch oven

And drain off any excess fat then return Dutch oven to stove then add olive oil, sweet butter over medium heat then add your garlic, ginger then stir cook for 3 minutes

Then add your onions, hot peppers, pine nuts, mushrooms then stir cook for 6 minutes then add your sausage, lobster meat, crab meat, shrimp, tomatoes, chicken stock

Fresh herbs, white wine, cognac stir then reduce heat to low and over and simmer for 12 minutes then remove from heat add your pasta toss or stir with a spoon until

Pasta is well coated then season to taste with kosher salt and ground white pepper. To serve spoon pasta on to dinner plates then garnish with parmesan cheese shavings.

CURRIED RICE WITH GINGER, PEPPERS, BEEF, AND SHRIMP

Makes 6 servings

Ingredients:

2	lb pepper steak, slice thin
2	lb bag 16/20 jumbo shrimp cleaned, shelled, butter flied
1	medium red bell pepper, seeded and diced
1	medium green bell pepper, seeded and diced
1	medium yellow bell pepper, seeded and diced
6	medium Serrano peppers, seeded and diced
1	medium Vidalia onion, diced small
1	medium Bermuda onion, diced small
3	medium plum tomatoes, medium diced
2	tablespoons yellow curry powder
2	tablespoons fresh ginger, minced
2	tablespoons fresh garlic cloves, minced
2	tablespoons fresh lemon grass, finely chopped
3	cups wild mushrooms, sliced
⅓	cup olive oil
5	cups beef stock or water
2 ¼	cups white rice
	New groove house seasoning blend, to taste
1	bunch fresh cilantro chopped, for garnish

Procedure:

In a large 5 qt Dutch oven over medium heat and olive oil then sliced pepper steak stir cook for 5 minutes then add your diced peppers, diced onions, garlic, ginger, lemon grass

Sliced wile mushrooms, diced plum tomatoes, curry powder then stir cook for 5 minutes then add beef stock or water then rice then stir cover and simmer for 10 minutes over medium low heat when uncover rice mixture then add your jumbo shrimp stir then cover then simmer for 10 minutes then remove curry rice from heat let rice stand covered for 5 minutes then season to taste with New Groove House Seasoning Blend to serve curry rice spoon rice on to dinner plates then garnish with chopped cilantro then serve.

ROASTED WHITE CORN AND RED BEANS

WITH JALAPENO AND ANAHEIM CHILE PEPPER RICE LACED WITH COGNAC RUM AND TEQUILA

Makes 6 servings

Ingredients:

- 3 ½ cups basmati rice
- 5 cups chicken stock
- 1 cup Hennessy cognac
- 1 cup Jose Cuervo gold tequila
- 1 cup Bacardi dark rum,
- 3 tablespoons fresh ginger root peeled, finely chopped
- 3 tablespoons fresh lemon grass, finely chopped
- 2 medium fresh Anaheim Chile peppers, seeded and chopped
- 3 medium fresh Jalapeno Chile peppers seeded and chopped
- 2 12 oz cans red beans, well drained
- 1 16 oz bag frozen white corn kernels season with s&p, roasted
- 3 tablespoons sweet butter, add to rice
  New groove Caribbean jerk seasoning, to taste

Procedure:

First pre-heat oven at 350°F then place your white corn on a baking sheet then season corn with kosher salt and ground black pepper then place in oven roast corn for about 12 minutes then remove corn from oven put aside and let cool. Then in a large 8 qt Dutch oven over high heat combine chicken stock, cognac, dark rum, 1 cup Jose Cuervo gold tequila and bring to a boil then reduce heat to medium low heat then add your lemon grass, ginger, garlic, jalapeno Chile peppers Anaheim Chile peppers, red beans, and roasted white corn, basmati rice then stir then cover and cook until liquid has been absorbed and rice is tender then remove from heat season to taste with Caribbean jerk seasoning And finish with 3 tablespoons sweet butter stir well. Serve with grilled steak, chicken, pork fish, or seafood.

ROASTED WHITE CORN AND RED BEANS WITH HABENERO RICE LACED WITH COCONUT RUM AND PEPPAR VODKA

Makes 6 servings

Ingredients:
- 3 cups basmati rice
- 5 cups chicken stock
- ⅓ cup Cruzan Coconut Rum
- ⅓ cup Absolut Peppar Vodka
- ½ cup White wine
- 2 tablespoons fresh ginger root, peeled and chopped
- 2 tablespoons fresh garlic, peeled and chopped
- 3 tablespoons fresh lemon grass, finely chopped for garnish
- 3 fresh Habanero Chile, seeded and chopped for garnish
- 1 16 oz can red beans, drained
- 1 bag frozen fresh sweet white corn, roasted
- Season with salt and pepper
- Season with Caribbean jerk seasoning
- 2 tablespoons sweet cream butter

Procedure:

In a large 8 quart dutch oven combine chicken stock, white wine, coconut rum and pepper vodka. Bring to a boil. Reduce heat to medium low heat and add in ginger, garlic, lemon grass, chilies, red beans corn and rice. Season with salt and pepper. Cook until liquid has been absorbed and rice is tender. Remove from heat and season with Caribbean jerk. Finish with one to two tablespoons of sweet cream butter mix well. Serve with grilled beef, chicken, pork, fish or seafood. Garnish with finely chopped lemon grass and Habanero chile peppers.

NEW GROOVE PIZZA DOUGH

Makes 2 Large Pies

Ingredients:

4 ¼	cups all purpose flour
1	teaspoon salt
1 ½ - 2 ¼	cups warm water, 110F to 115F
2	oz dry yeast
¼	cup olive oil
¼	cup sugar or honey
⅔	cup freshly grated pecorino cheese

Procedure:

First, in a large mixing bowl add flour and salt, and then stir. Then in a medium-size bowl add water, olive oil, yeast sugar or honey. Stir. Let stand for 2 minutes, and then add yeast mixture to flour. Then, with a mixer fitted with a dough hook added to the mixing bowl, knead dough until smooth, about 5 minutes. Then add a little olive oil to a large bowl. Add dough. Turn to coat. Cover in a warm place. Dough rises in an hour. Then transfer dough to a floured board and divide pizza dough. Roll out dough, and then transfer to pizza pan. Brush dough with a little olive oil, then top with grated cheese. Place pizza dough in oven. Pre-bake dough at 450 for about 8 minutes. Makes two large pies.

SPICY FUSION-STYLE ITALIAN BREADSTICKS

Ingredients:

3 ½	cups all purpose flour
2	1oz packages active dry yeast
2 ½	teaspoons salt
¼	cup honey
1	bunch of fresh thyme
4	Jalapeno peppers, seeded, finely chopped
4	Red Thai chilies, seeded, finely chopped
2	cups Italian blend cheese, shredded
¼	cup olive oil
1 ½	cups warm water 115° F

For Glaze

3   eggs beaten with 3 tbsp water

For Dusting

New groove house seasoning optional

¼   cup black sesame seeds

¼   cup white sesame seeds

Procedure:

In large bowl combine flour, salt, fresh thyme, jalapeno peppers, Thai chilies, Italian blend cheese stir to blend then in a medium size bowl combine warm water, yeast, olive oil, honey stir then add to four mixture. Stir with a wooden spoon or with a stand up mixer with a paddle attachment mix well then turn out dough on a floured board knead for 7 minutes then put dough in large greased bowl let it rest for 35 minutes then divide dough into 4 pieces then preheat your oven at 450°F on a floured board roll 1 piece dough into ¼ inch thick into a rectangle then cut dough crosswise into 12 1 inch wide strips twist each strip place on a greased baking sheet brush bread sticks with egg glaze. Sprinkle with New Groove House Seasoning, black sesame seeds, white sesame seeds bake for 15 to 20 minutes or until golden brown. Makes 4 dozen breadsticks.

NEW GROOVE PIZZA SAUCE

Makes 1 gallon

Ingredients:
- 1 medium-size carrot, peeled, chopped
- 3 celery stalks, chopped
- 1 medium-size onion, chopped
- ¼ cup olive oil
- 2 tbsp chopped garlic
- ¼ cup red wine
- ¼ cup sugar
- Salt and pepper to taste
- 2 tbsp dried thyme
- 2 tbsp dried basil
- 2 tbsp dried oregano
- 1 tbsp crushed red pepper flakes
- 2 bay leafs
- 1 tbsp dried marjoram
- 1 tbsp dried tarragon
- 1 28 oz can whole plum tomatoes
- 1 28 oz can crushed tomatoes
- 1 ¼ cups water

Procedure:

First, in a 4-qt saucepan over medium heat add olive oil, then carrots, celery, onion. Cook for 15 minutes, and then add whole tomatoes, water crushed tomatoes, garlic, and sugar, wine, thyme, basil, marjoram, tarragon, oregano, crushed red pepper. Reduce heat to low simmer for 25 minutes and then, with a hand mixer, blend sauce until smooth. Season to taste with salt and pepper. Add bay leafs and simmer for another 35 minutes. Remove from heat and discard bay leafs before using.

NEW GROOVE PIZZA DOUGH 2

Makes 2 large pies

Ingredients:
- 5 cups all purpose flour
- 1 teaspoon salt
- 1 ½ to 2 ½ cups warm water, 110F to 115F
- 3 oz dry yeast
- ¼ cup olive oil
- ¼ cup sugar or honey
- ½ cup grated parmesan cheese
- ½ cup grated Romano cheese
- ½ cup grated mozzarella cheese
- 3 tbsp crushed red pepper flakes
- ⅔ cup freshly grated pecorino cheese

Procedure:

First, in a mixing bowl add flour and salt, and then the parmesan, Romano, mozzarella cheeses, crushed red pepper flakes. Stir. Then in a medium-size bowl add water, olive oil, yeast, sugar or honey. Stir. Let stand for 2 minutes, and then add yeast mixture to flour. With a mixer fitted with a dough hook, knead dough until smooth, about 5 minutes, and then add a little olive oil to a large bowl, then add dough. Turn to coat. Cover in a warm place. Dough rises in an hour. Transfer dough to a floured board, and then divide pizza dough. Roll out dough. Transfer to pizza pan. Brush dough with a little olive oil, then top with grated pecorino cheese. Place dough in oven. Pre-bake dough at 450F for about 8 minutes. Makes two large pies.

NEW GROOVE SAUSAGE AND MUSHROOM PIZZA

Makes 2 large pies

Ingredients:
- 2 cups wild mushrooms, sliced
- 7 fresh plum tomatoes, diced
- 1 bunch fresh cinnamon basil, chopped
- 1 bunch fresh marjoram, chopped
- 1 bunch fresh cilantro, chopped
- ½ pound Italian hot sausage casing removed, cooked and crumbled
- ½ pound Italian sweet sausage casing removed, cooked and crumbled
- ⅓ cup ex virgin olive oil, sprinkle over tomato
- ¼ cup fresh ginger, peeled and chopped
- ¼ cup garlic cloves, chopped
- 1 medium red onion, sliced
- 3 medium size Anaheim chili peppers, seeded and sliced
- 2 cups Romano cheese, grated
- 2 cups Monterrey pepper jack cheese, grated
- 2 cups mozzarella cheese, grated
- New groove house seasoning to taste

Procedure:

Take prepared pizza dough and roll out. Place them on the pan and brush them with olive oil. Top with grated pecorino cheese. Pre-bake at 450°F for 8 minutes then remove pizza dough from oven. Add toppings and tomatoes. Season with new groove house seasoning or salt and pepper. Sprinkle with olive oil, garlic, ginger, wild mushrooms, red onion, marjoram, basil, cilantro, sausages, Anaheim chili peppers, Romano cheese, pepper jack cheese and mozzarella cheese. Bake at 450°F for 16 minutes then remove pizza from oven. Cut and serve. Makes two large pizzas.

NEW YORK STYLE NEW GROOVE PIZZA

Makes 2 large pies

Ingredients:

- 1 pound Italian hot sausage casing removed, cooked and crumbled
- 2 medium size Poblano chili peppers, seeded and chopped
- 4 shallots, chopped fine
- 6 chanterelle mushrooms, stems removed, diced
- ⅓ cup garlic cloves, chopped
- ⅓ cup extra virgin olive oil
- 1 ½ cups mozzarella cheese, grated
- 2 cups pecorino Romano cheese, grated
- 2 cups Fusion pizza sauce, prepared as directed
- 2 large Fusion pizza dough, prepared as directed
- 2 cups pine nuts, toasted
- 2 medium size Anaheim chili peppers, seeded and chopped
- 1 bunch fresh cilantro, chopped

Procedure:

Pre-heat oven at 450°F. Take two prepared pizza dough's and roll out. Brush pizza dough's with olive oil and top with garlic and 1 cup pecorino Romano cheese. Pre-bake pizza dough at 450°F for 8 minutes. Remove from oven then top with sausage, chili peppers shallots, cilantro, pine nuts, mushrooms, pizza sauce, mozzarella cheese and the remaining pecorino Romano cheese. Bake for another 12 to 15 minutes then remove pizzas from oven. Cut and serve. Makes two large pizzas.

NEW GROOVE SURF N TURF PIZZA

Makes 2 large pies

Ingredients:

1 ½	pounds 16/20 jumbo shrimp, shelled and cleaned
2	1 pound cans lobster meat, drained
1	pound sweet Italian sausage casing removed, cooked and crumbled
3	fresh Italian peppers, seeded and sliced thin
4	fresh Serrano chili peppers, seeded and sliced thin
1	cup pine nuts
1	bunch fresh tarragon, chopped
1	bunch fresh cilantro, chopped
1	bunch fresh lemon basil, chopped
4	cups Italian blend cheese, shredded
	Fusion pizza sauce recipe, prepared as directed

Procedure:

Take two prepared pizza dough's and roll out. Brush pizza dough's with a little olive oil. Top with some Italian blend cheese. Pre-bake for 8 minutes at 450°F. Remove pizza dough's from oven then add sauce, chopped cilantro, lemon basil, tarragon, pine nuts, lobster meat, shrimp, sausage Italian peppers, Serrano chili peppers and Italian blend cheese. Return pizzas to the oven and bake at 450°F for 16 minutes. Remove pizzas from oven. Cut and serve. Makes two large pizzas.

TURKEY SAUSAGE PIZZA
WITH BLUE CHEESE, JALAPENO'S AND SERRANO PEPPERS

Makes 2 large pies

Ingredients:
- 1 pound hot Italian turkey sausage casing removed, cooked and crumbled
- 1 bunch fresh sage, chopped
- 1 bunch fresh oregano, chopped
- 1 bunch fresh chervil, chopped
- 1 medium size red onion, sliced
- 4 fresh Jalapeño Chile peppers, seeded and sliced
- 4 fresh Serrano Chile peppers, seeded and sliced
- 2 cups blue cheese, crumbled
- 2 cups Italian blend cheese, grated
- 2 cups mozzarella cheese, grated
- Fusion pizza sauce recipe, prepared as directed
- Fusion pizza dough recipe, prepared as directed

Procedure:

Pre-heat oven at 450°F. Take prepared pizza dough and roll it out. Place on pizza pans brushed with olive oil. Top with grated pecorino cheese then pre-bake pizza dough at 450°F for 8 minutes. Remove pizza from oven and add pizza sauce. Add sausage, sage, oregano, chervil red onion, jalapeño Chile peppers, Serrano chili peppers, mozzarella cheese, Italian blend cheese and blue cheese. Bake at 450°F for 15 minutes then remove pizza from oven. Cut and serve. Makes two pizzas.

Main Dishes

Beef, Chicken, Pork, Veal

Chicken...

You may hear the word "chicken" and think BORING!!! Well, not so! I use fresh high quality chicken. My dishes are not the lease bit boring. In fact, they are flavor-intensive, all dressed-up and ready to take you out on an exotic "east meet west" a fusion style dining experience.

Veal...

When you have a taste for something other than chicken, but not the heartiness of beef – then veal is the choice for you. I bring the very best in high quality veal dishes. Packed with all-natural, fresh ingredients, my veal creations will keep you coming back for more.

Beef...

Beef is and always has been the hearty/satisfying choice. Who can't pass up a juicy, grilled to perfection NY strip steak, a Kansas City Strip Steak? How about a tender Filet Mignon pan seared just to your liking? My beef dishes are sure to wow you with the freshest ingredients and fusion flavors that are BIG and **BOLD**.

Pork...

Once considered the other "white meat", my pork dishes will make your mouth sing. I use top grade, choice cut tenderloins in my pork dishes. Then I fuse them with common to exotic fruits, vegetables herbs spices and a vest selection of flavorings. The result is a mouth-watering symphony of flavor.

Fish & Seafood...

Always a favorite, I bring you the very best the oceans and seas have to offer. From fresh lobster and jumbo lump crab meat from the waters of Maine to South Africa to fresh prawns and scallops from Maryland to the Gulf of Mexico and a wide/vast variety of fish from the Atlantic and Pacific Oceans. My signature seafood dishes showcase what my style of fusion is all about. Like my other dishes, I use only top quality choice, fresh seafood and fish. Then I marry them with common to exotic ingredients herbs, spices oils liqueurs and flavorings to create a fusion inspired culinary masterpiece.

EAST - WEST STYLE STUFFED CHICKEN BREAST

Makes 4 servings

Ingredients:

- ½ cup olive oil
- 1 ¼ cups wild mushrooms, finely chopped
- 1 package fresh baby spinach, chopped
- 1 bunch fresh tarragon, chopped
- 1 bunch fresh lemon basil, chopped
- 1 bunch fresh lemon thyme
- 5 fresh Thai Red Chile peppers, seeded and chopped
- 5 medium shallots, finely chopped
- 1 ¼ cups hazelnuts, chopped
- ¼ cup fresh garlic, finely chopped
- 3 tablespoons fresh ginger, finely chopped
- ¼ cup Dekuyper hazelnut liquor
- ¼ cup Champagne
- ¼ cup Bacardi Black rum
- 1 ¼ cups cream cheese, room temp
- ½ cup green onions, chopped
- ½ cup Dijon mustard, spread on chicken
- 3 pounds chicken breast halves, cleaned
- Salt and pepper, to taste

Procedure:

First pre heat oven at 450°F then in a large frying pan over medium head add oil, hazelnut liquor, champagne, Black rum, then garlic, ginger, Thai Chile peppers

Shallots, Hazelnuts, mushrooms. Then saute for about 5 minutes then remove heat cool slightly then in a large mixing bowl combine baby spinach, tarragon, lemon basil

Lemon thyme, cream cheese, green onions. Then fold in mushroom hazelnut ginger garlic Thai Chile peppers mixture season to taste with salt & pepper then run fingers

Under the skin to make pocket then spread cream cheese mixture between skin and meat then place chicken breast on baking sheet and spread with Dijon mustard

On chicken then bake at 450°F for about 20 to 25 minutes then remove from oven

Then serve chicken with vegetables mashed potatoes or with roasted potatoes or with rice

NEW GROOVE CHICKEN N PEACHES TWISTED

Ingredients:

- 5   Boneless Chicken Breast cleaned and seasoned with Kosher salt and Ground White pepper
- 5   fresh garlic cloves chopped
- 1   cup Roasted Plum Tomatoes Diced
- 1   cup sliced Almonds Toasted
- 1 ½   cups sliced Yellow Peaches
- 2   Teaspoons crushed Red pepper flakes
- 2   Tablespoons Flat leaf Parsley chopped
- 2   Tablespoons Sweet basil chopped
- 2   Tablespoons oregano chopped
- 5   Jumbo eggs beaten
- 2 ¼   cups All-purpose flour
- 3   cups Buttermilk
- ½   cup olive oil
- 1   stick sweet butter
- 1 ¼   cup's chicken stock
- 1 ¼   Amaretto Liquor

Kosher salt and Ground white pepper to taste

Procedure:

First clean and seasoned your chicken breast with kosher salt and coarse ground white pepper. Then dredge chicken in flour then in the beaten egg mixture. Then in a large 8 qt Dutch oven over medium high heat add your olive oil and sweet butter then add your chicken breast then cook 5 minutes per side then place your chicken breast in a oval dish. Then in the same 8 at Dutch oven, add your garlic, Roasted tomatoes, sliced toasted almonds, red pepper flakes, stir cook for 3 minutes then add your chicken stock, Buttermilk, Amaretto Liquor then simmer for 15 minutes. Then stir in parsley, Basil oregano, Yellow peaches then remove from heat then season to taste with kosher salt and ground white pepper then pour sauce over chicken breast then serve.

NEW GROOVE STUFFED PORK CHOPS

Ingredients:
- 6   1 inch thick pork Chops put on a slit in the side to make pocket then season pork chops with kosher salt N coarse ground black pepper
- Black pepper

For stuffing
- 1   lb can lobster meat chopped
- 1   lb can Jumbo Lump crab meat
- 2   Italian peppers seeded medium diced
- 1   medium Vidalia onion medium diced
- ⅓   cup pinenuts
- 1   cup Parmesan cheese
- ⅓   cup Champagne
- 3   Jumbo eggs
- 2   cups fresh bread crumbs
- 1   Tablespoon fresh flat leaf parsley chopped
- 1   Tablespoon fresh oregano chopped
- 1   Tablespoon fresh thyme
- 1   Tablespoon fresh Basil
- ⅓   cup Olive oil to sear pork chops

For Breading Station
- 2   cups All-purpose flour
- 5   Jumbo eggs beaten
- 2   cups milk
- 5   cups fresh bread crumbs
- 3   Tablespoons fresh flat leaf parsley chopped
- 3   Tablespoons fresh oregano chopped
- 3   Tablespoons fresh Thyme over
- 3   Tablespoons fresh basil chopped

Procedure:

First make a slit in the side of each pork chop to make pocket for stuffing then season pork chops with salt N pepper then in a large mixing bowl combine Vidalia onion Italian peppers, pinenuts lobster meat, Jumbo lump crab meat bread crumbs, Jumbo eggs parmesan cheese champagne and one tablespoon of each parsley, thyme oregano, basil then mix well then stuff each pork chop. Then in a large bowl combine flour. Then another large bowl combine eggs, milk. In another large bowl combine bread crumbs, parsley, oregano, thyme, basil. Then dredge each pork chop in flour then in egg milk mixture then in bread crumbs then put aside then in a large saute pan over medium high heat add olive oil then add 3 pork chops cook for 2 minutes on each side then place on baking sheet then do the remaining pork chops place pork chops in oven bake at 350°F for about 25 minutes or until done.

Serve 6 people

NEW GROOVE VEAL MEDALIONS TWISTED

Ingredients:

- 14 pieces Milkfed baby Veal medalions
- 2 cups buttermilk
- 7 Plum Tomatoes diced
- 2 1lb package crawfish tail meat
- 2 medium size eggplant diced
- 2 medium size Vidalia onions diced
- 8 cloves garlic chopped
- 2 lbs Baby Broccolini Blanched
- ½ cup pinenuts
- 4 fresh Jalapeno chili peppers seeded and sliced
- ½ cup Olive oil
- 5 Tablespoons Sweet Stock
- ¼ lb pancetta Bacon Sliced thin then diced
- 1 cup Veal Stock
- ⅓ cup Port Demi
- ⅓ cup Port Wine
- 2 cup All-purpose flour
- 7 Jumbo eggs beaten
- 1 small bunch flat leaf parsley chopped
- 1 small bunch marjeram chopped

Kosher salt & corase ground black pepper to taste.

Procedure:

First in a bowl add buttermilk then add your veal let veal marinate for 30 minutes then dredge veal in flour then in eggs in a large 8 quart Dutch oven over medium high heat add olive oil sweet butter then add veal cook for 3 minutes per side the place veal on a large platter keep warm then in the same Dutch oven add pancetta bacon onions, garlic pinenuts eggplant Jalapeno chili pepers stir cook for 4 minutes then add your blanched baby brocollini, plum tomatoes crawfish tail meat Veal stock, port-Demi, port Wine stir simmer for 14 minutes then stir in parsley, marjoram season to taste with Kosher salt & coarse ground Black pepper then pour sauce over veal serve

Serves 5 people

FUSION STYLE SPICY STEAK PORTUGUESE
LACED WITH TEQUILA AND BOURBON

Makes 4 servings

Ingredients:
- 4   12 oz New York strip steaks trimmed, seasoned
- ¼   cup olive oil
- 5   fresh shallots, diced
- 4   tablespoons garlic cloves, finely chopped
- 3   tablespoons ginger, finely chopped
- 3   fresh red jalapeno Chile peppers, seeded finely chop
- 3   fresh Thai Chile peppers, seeded finely chop
- 6   medium plum tomatoes, diced
- ¼   cup Champagne
- 2   bay leaves
- 1   teaspoon Chinese 5 spice
- 1   teaspoon Worcestershire sauce
- ¼   teaspoon ground saffron
- ¼   cup Jose Cuervo tequila
- ¼   cup knob creek bourbon

   New groove house seasoning blend or salt & pepper, to taste

Procedure:

In a large sauté pan over medium heat add olive oil then add steaks seasoned with new groove house seasoning blend or salt & pepper then cook steaks 3 minutes per side.

Then add shallots, ginger, garlic, red jalapeno Chile peppers, Thai Chile peppers, plum tomatoes, bay leaves, Chinese 5 spice, Worcestershire sauce, saffron, Champagne, bourbon, tequila. Stir bring to a boil then reduce heat then simmer for 10 minutes then remove heat seasoned to taste with new groove house seasoning blend or Salt & pepper. Then transfer steaks to a large serving platter then spoon sauce over steaks serve with steam vegetables, rice, mashed potatoes, or roasted potatoes.

GRILLED RIB EYE STEAKS WITH A GARLIC, MUSTARD SAUCE

Makes 2 servings

Ingredients:
- 2   6 oz boneless rib-eye steaks, brushed with oil
- 4   tablespoons cracked black pepper, season steaks
- 3   tablespoons kosher salt, season steaks
- ¼   cup olive oil, brush on steaks

For garlic mustard sauce
- ¼   cup garlic cloves, chopped
- ⅓   cup Cabernet Sauvignon add to sauce
- ⅓   cup Champagne add to sauce
- ⅓   cup Bacardi gold rum add to sauce
- 1   cup beef stock or chicken stock, add to sauce
- ⅓   cup Dijon mustard, add to sauce
- 2   sticks sweet cream butter, whisk in sauce
- 4   tablespoons fresh cilantro, chopped
-      Salt and pepper, to taste

Procedure:

First in a large 4 qt sauce pan over medium heat add beef stock or chicken stock, garlic, champagne, gold rum cabernet sauvignon, Dijon mustard then bring sauce to a boil then whisk until blended then reduce heat to medium cook for 3 minutes then remove from heat then add sweet butter whisk until melted then stir

In cilantro then put aside then brush rib eye steaks with olive oil on both sides then season steaks with cracked black pepper and kosher salt on both sides

Then grill rib-eye steaks to desired doneness. Then transfer rib eye steaks to a large serving platter then spoon sauce over rib eye steaks. Serve with Steam vegetables and roasted potatoes or baked potatoes.

NEW YORK STRIP STEAKS
WITH A THAI MARINADE FUSION STYLE

Makes 5 servings

Ingredients:

5   18 oz New York strip steaks (Angus), cleaned and seasoned

For Thai marinade

- ⅔ cup olive oil, mix together
- 4 fresh Thai red Chile peppers seeded, chopped, mix together
- 3 tablespoons fresh ginger chopped, mix together
- 3 tablespoons fresh garlic cloves chopped, mix together
- 3 tablespoons fresh shallots chopped, mix together
- 3 tablespoons fresh cilantro chopped, mix together
- 3 tablespoons fresh lemon thyme, mix together
- 3 tablespoons fresh Thai basil chopped, mix together
- 3 tablespoons Habanero Chile peppers seeded chopped, mix together
- 3 tablespoons Serrano chile peppers seeded chopped, mix together
- ½ cup Hennessey cognac mix together
- ½ cup French apple brandy (calvados) mix together
- ½ cup Cruzan vanilla rum mix together
- ½ cup honey, mix together
- ⅓ cup grapefruit juice, mix together
- ⅓ cup orange juice, mix together
- 2 tablespoons grapefruit zest, mix together
- 2 tablespoons orange zest, mix together
- 2 teaspoons paprika, mix together

1	teaspoon ground allspice, mix together
1	teaspoon ground nutmeg, mix together
1	teaspoon ground cinnamon, mix together
	Salt and pepper or new groove house seasoning, season steaks
1	medium grapefruit peeled sliced, for garnish
1	medium orange peeled sliced, for garnish
2	tablespoons grapefruit zest, for garnish
2	tablespoons orange zest, for garnish

Procedure:

First clean New York strip steaks then season steaks with salt pepper or new groove house seasoning blend on both sides. Meanwhile in a large food processor combine all ingredients for marinade olive oil, Thai Chile peppers, Habenero Chile peppers, Serrano Chile peppers, ginger, garlic, shallots, cilantro, rum, honey, grapefruit juice, orange juice, Thai basil, lemon thyme, calvados, cognac nutmeg, cinnamon, grapefruit zest, orange zest, paprika, allspice, blend for one minute or until smooth. Place steaks into a large container and pour marinade over the top and cover chill for 4 to 5 hours before grilling after grilling steaks then transfer steaks to a large serving platter garnish with thin slices of grapefruit and orange and sprinkle with grapefruit and orange zest. Serve with corn on the cob and baked potatoes.

NEW GROOVE FUSION TANGERINE STEAK

Makes 4 servings

Ingredients:
- 4   12 oz New York strip steak trimmed, seasoned
- 3   tablespoons ginger, finely chopped
- ¼   cup Canola oil
- 1   teaspoon ground cinnamon
- ½   teaspoon ground nutmeg
- 3   tablespoons garlic cloves, finely chopped
- 5   fresh Thai Chilie peppers, finely chopped
- 5   tablespoons tangerine peel, grated
- 1   cup tangerine juice
- 2   11 oz cans tangerine sections, drained
- ⅓   cup Absolut Mandarin vodka
- ⅓   cup Absolut Peppar vodka
-      New groove house seasoning blend or salt & pepper, cto taste

Procedure:

First season strip steaks with new groove house seasoning bland or salt & pepper then in a large 8 qt Dutch oven over medium high heat add Canola oil then add strip steaks cook steaks 3 minutes per side then remove steaks then add ginger, garlic, nutmeg, cinnamon, tangerine peel, Thai chilie peppers. Cook for 3 minutes then add tangerine Juice, Absolut Mandarin Vodka, Absolut Peppar Vodka and then return steaks to Dutch oven reduce heat to medium simmer for 10 minutes then add tangerine sections stir then remove from Heat season to taste with new groove house seasoning blend or salt & pepper. Then place strip steaks on plates then spoon tangerine sections and juice over steaks then serve.

With steam vegetables, rice, roasted potatoes or mashed potatoes.

NEW GROOVE
FIREY STEAK PROVENCALE

Makes 4 servings

Ingredients:

- 4   12 oz New York strip steaks trimmed, seasoned
- ¼   cup Canela oil
- 6   medium shallots, finely chopped
- 6   fresh garlic cloves, finely chopped
- 3   fresh Habanero Chile peppers seeded, finely chopped
- 3   fresh Thai Chile peppers seeded, finely chopped
- 3   fresh green Serrano Chile peppers seeded, finely chopped
- ¼   cup Jose Cuervo gold tequila
- ¼   cup Jack Daniels bourbon
- ¼   cup Don Q 151 rum
-         Salt and pepper, to taste
-         For yogurt sauce
- 1   quart vanilla yogurt
- 2   fresh Thai Chile peppers seeded, finely chopped
- 2   tablespoons fresh chervil, chopped
- ¼   cup Jack Daniels bourbon
- ⅓   cup honey

Procedure:

First in a large bowl combine vanilla yogurt, Thai Chile peppers, chervil, honey, bourbon mix well then chill then in a large sauté pan over medium high heat add Canela oil, then add your steaks season with new groove house reasoning blend or salt & pepper cook steaks 3 minutes per side then remove steaks place on a plate

Then add shallots, garlic, habanero chili peppers, Thai Chile peppers, green Serrano Chile peppers cook for 3 minutes then remove from heat add steaks, bourbon 151 Rum, Jose Cuervo gold tequila. Then return sauté pan to heat then with a long stem match ignite alcohol then gently shake pan until flame goes out then remove from heat season

With salt & pepper to taste. Then place your finish steaks on a large serving platter then serve steaks with yogurt sauce. With steam vegetables rice, roasted potatoes

Or mashed potatoes.

CRAZY ZANZIBAR FUSION NEW YORK STRIP STEAKS
WITH GRAND MARNIER AND CITRON VODKA

Makes 4 servings

Ingredients:

4	12 oz New York strip steaks trimmed, seasoned
4	fresh shallots, chopped
7	fresh garlic cloves, minced
1	cup ruby red grapefruit juice
⅓	cup dried cranberries
⅓	cup pine nuts, toasted
¼	cup olive oil
¼	cup Grand Marnier
¼	cup absolut citron vodka
5	fresh green Serrano Chile peppers, seeded finely chopped
	New groove seasoning or salt & pepper, to taste

Procedure:

First season steaks with new groove house seasoning blend or salt pepper then in large sauté pan over medium high heat add olive oil then steaks cook for 3 minutes per side

Then remove steaks place on platter put aside then add your garlic, shallots, Serrano Chile peppers, cook for 3 minutes then return steaks to the sauté pan

Then add dried cranberries, pine nuts then, grapefruit juice, citron vodka, Grand Marnier. Reduce heat simmer for 10 minutes season to taste with new groove seasoning blend or salt & pepper

Then remove from heat serve. Then place steaks on a large serving platter then spoon sauce over steaks serve with vegetables, rice, mashed potatoes, or roasted potatoes

NEW YORK STRIP STEAK AND SHRIMP HOOK-UP DONE NEW GROOVE STYLE

Makes 2 servings

Ingredients:

- 2   14 oz Angus beef strip steaks, seasoned with s&p
- 1   cup portabella mushrooms, sliced
- 1   large Vidalia onion, sliced
- 3   tablespoons fresh garlic cloves, chopped
- 2   tablespoons fresh ginger, chopped
- ½   pound 16/20 jumbo shrimp, peeled and deveined
- ¼   cup Champagne, optional
- ¼   cup Bacardi gold rum
- ¼   cup Hennessey cognac
- ¼   cup peanut oil

Season to taste with new groove house seasoning or salt & pepper

Procedure:

First pre-heat oven to 350°F then in a large sauté pan over medium high heat add peanut oil then add seasoned steaks sear steaks on both sides for 2 minutes then place steaks on sheet tray finish steaks in oven cook your steaks how done you like your steaks then in the same sauté pan onion, portabella mushrooms then sauté for 3 minutes then add ginger, garlic champagne, shrimp, rum, cognac cook for 4 minutes season to taste with new groove house seasoning or salt & pepper remove steaks from oven place steaks on a large platter then pour.

Shrimp & onion mushroom mixture over steaks then serve with steam vegetables, roasted potatoes, or baked potatoes.

MOROCCAN STYLE NEW GROOVE STEAKS
WITH COGNAC AND CALVADOS

Makes 4 servings

Ingredients:

4	12 oz New York strip steak trimmed, seasoned
¼	cup peanut oil
4	tablespoons garlic cloves
2	tablespoons ginger, finely chopped
2	tablespoons lemon grass, finely chopped
¼	cup shallots, finely chopped
1	tablespoon ground cinnamon
1	tablespoon ground nutmeg
¼	teaspoon ground mace
¼	teaspoon ground saffron
1 ¼	cups hazelnuts, chopped and toasted
3	tablespoons fresh chervil, chopped
⅓	cup Hennessey cognac
⅓	cup French apple brandy (calvados)
1 ⅔	cups apple juice
	New groove house seasoning blend or salt & pepper, to taste

Procedure:

First season steaks with new groove house seasoning blend or kosher salt & ground black pepper then in a large 8 qt Dutch oven over medium high heat add peanut oil then add your steaks cook for 4 minutes per side then remove steaks place on a large plate then add garlic, ginger, shallots, lemon grass, cinnamon, nutmeg mace, saffron stir cook for 3 minutes then add your steaks back to the Dutch oven then add hazelnuts, apple juice, cognac, French apple brandy then lower heat to medium low

Then simmer for 10 minutes then season to taste with new groove house seasoning blend or kosher salt & ground black pepper then remove from heat to serve place steaks

On plates then spoon sauce over steaks serve with steam vegetables, rice or roasted potatoes.

SAUTEED CHICKEN BREAST
WITH ALMONDS, HAZELNUTS AND PLUMS

Makes 5 servings

Ingredients:

1	cup blanched almonds, toasted
½	cup sesame seeds, toasted
1	cup hazelnuts, chopped and toasted
4	medium Vidalia onions, sliced
½	cup safflower oil
4	pounds boneless chicken breast seasoned with s&p, cleaned
2	cups dried plums
2	tablespoons ground cinnamon
1	tablespoon ground turmeric
1	bunch fresh tarragon, chopped
3	tablespoons lemon grass, finely chopped
4	tablespoons fresh garlic cloves, finely chopped
3	small fresh Thai chili peppers, seeded and minced
2	cups chicken stock or water
2	cups Hennessey cognac, add to stock
2	cups Cruzan vanilla rum, add to stock
⅓	cup honey, drizzle over chicken
	New groove house seasoning, season to taste

Procedure:

First toast the almonds, sesame seeds, hazelnuts in a large sauté pan over medium high heat for about 5 minutes then set aside then in a large 8 qt Dutch oven over medium high heat add safflower oil, Thai chili peppers, lemon grass, garlic, onions then stir cook for 5 minutes then add chicken breast cook for 5 minutes then add dried plums

Cinnamon, turmeric, chicken stock or water, cognac, vanilla rum, tarragon, stir then bring to a boil then reduce heat to low then cover cook for 25 minutes them remove from heat season to taste with salt & pepper then place chicken, plums and pan juices on a large serving platter then drizzle honey over chicken then sprinkle hazelnuts, sesame

Seeds, almonds on top.

SPICY-HOT GINGER-CITRUS, CHICKEN AND SHRIMP

LACED WITH GINGER BRANDY AND PINEAPPLE RUM

Makes 5 servings

Ingredients:

2	pounds 16/20 jumbo shrimp, cleaned butter flied
5	medium boneless chicken breast, cleaned
7	medium garlic cloves, finely chopped
5	tablespoons fresh ginger, finely chopped
1	stick sweet cream butter, softened
⅓	cup olive oil, add to butter
3	small Thai Chile peppers, seeded and minced
3	small Jalapeno Chile peppers, seeded and minced
2	cups canned dice pineapple, small diced
1	tablespoon lemon zest, use a zester
1	tablespoon orange zest, use a zester
1	tablespoon lime zest, use a zester
⅓	cup Jacquin's ginger brandy
⅓	cup Cruzan pineapple rum
⅓	cup Cruzan citrus rum
1	small orange ½ wedges, sliced thin
1	small lime ½ wedges, sliced thin
1	small lemon ½ wedges, sliced thin
	Salt and pepper, to taste
4	tablespoons fresh cilantro leaves, garnish

Procedure:

In a large 8 qt Dutch oven over medium heat add olive oil, sweet butter, garlic, ginger chicken breast cook for 4 minutes per side then add jumbo shrimp, diced pineapple

Thai Chile peppers, jalapeno chili peppers, orange zest, lemon zest, lime zest, ginger brandy, pineapple rum, citrus rum stir cook for 6 minutes or until shrimp turn pink then season to taste with salt and pepper then place chicken breast on a large platter top with jumbo shrimp then spoon citrus mixture over chicken shrimp garnish with thin sliced orange

Lime, lemon wedges, and cilantro leaves.

PAN SEARED CHICKEN BREAST WITH BROCCOLI AND FUSILLI PASTA

Makes 5 servings

Ingredients:
- 1 pound broccoli florets, blanched
- 1 pound fusilli pasta, cooked and drained
- ⅓ cup olive oil
- ½ cup garlic cloves, chopped
- 5 medium shallots, chopped
- 4 tablespoons fresh ginger, chopped
- 3 tablespoons crushed red pepper flakes
- 1 cup pine nuts
- 2 cups chicken stock
- 2 cups Champagne
- 2 cups milk
- 2 cups heavy cream
- 1 bunch fresh chervil, chopped
- 2 cups Parmesan cheese, grated
- 3 pounds boneless chicken breast, cleaned & cooked
- 1 small red bell pepper diced, for garnish
- Salt and white pepper to taste
- ¼ cup olive oil, add to chicken

Procedure:

First in a large 5 qt Dutch oven over high heat bring 3 qts water to a boil then add broccoli florets cook for 3 minutes then shock broccoli florets in ice water

To stop cooking. Put aside then cook fusilli pasta then drain put aside then in a large sauté pan over medium high heat add 1/4 cup olive oil then add chicken breast pan sear

For 4 minutes per side then remove chicken breast from pan then slice into strips then put aside. Then in a large 5 qt Dutch oven over medium heat add 1/3 cup olive oil then

Shallots, ginger, garlic, crushed red pepper flakes, pine nuts then stir cook for 3 minutes then add champagne, chicken stock then simmer for 10 minutes then add milk heavy cream, parmesan cheese stir simmer for 10 minutes then stir in broccoli florets, sliced chicken breast, chervil stir then simmer for another 5 minutes then remove

From heat season to taste with salt & white pepper then pour sauce over pasta toss garnish with diced red bell pepper.

NEW GROOVE STYLE PAN SEARED CHICKEN BREASTS

WITH BLACK OLIVES, GARLIC AND CHAMPAGNE OVER PENNE

Makes 6 servings

Ingredients:

⅓	olive oil
¼	cup garlic cloves, chopped
4	medium shallots, chopped
3	pounds boneless chicken breast, cleaned
3	tablespoons fennel seeds, chopped
3	tablespoons orange zest
4	tablespoons fresh chervil, chopped
½	cup Champagne
1	cup black olives, sliced
1	pound penne pasta, cooked and drained
	New groove fusion house seasoning, season to taste

Procedure:

In a large sauté pan over medium high heat add olive oil then add chicken breast then pan sear chicken breast for 3 minutes per side then remove chicken breast from pan

Then slice chicken breast then return sliced chicken breast to sauté pan then add garlic, shallots, orange zest, fennel seed, chervil, black olives, champagne stir cook for 4 minutes

Then season to taste with new groove house seasoning then toss with penne pasta. Then serve

On dinner plates

CHEF GANT'S MANGO-ORANGE SAUTEED CHICKEN BREASTS
WITH MANGO RUM AND MANDARIN VODKA

Makes 6 servings

Ingredients:

6	8 oz boned and skinned chicken breast halves, cleaned
3 ½	tablespoons fresh ginger, finely chopped
4	tablespoons fresh garlic cloves, finely chopped
3	medium fresh shallots peeled, finely chopped
3	small Scotch bonnets chili peppers, seeded and minced
3	medium ripe mangos peeled, medium diced
⅓	cup fresh cilantro, finely chopped
1 ½	cups all-purpose flour seasoned with s&p, dredging chicken
1 ⅓	cups low salt chicken broth
1	cup Champagne
1	cup Cruzan mango rum
1	cup Absolut Mandarin vodka
2	11 oz can mandarin oranges, well drained
	Salt and pepper, to taste
½	cup olive oil

Procedure:

In a medium size bowl add 1 1/2 cups of flour seasoned with salt and pepper then dredge your chicken breast into the flour and shake off any excess flour then set aside

Next in a large 8 qt Dutch oven over medium heat add your olive oil then add your chicken breast cook 5 minutes per side then remove chicken breast place on a large platter cover and keep warm then in the same Dutch oven over medium heat add your shallots, garlic, ginger, scotch bonnets chili peppers stir cook for 4 minutes then add your low salt chicken broth champagne, mango rum, Mandarin vodka then stir then simmer for 20 minutes and then add your diced mangos, mandarin oranges stir then simmer for another 2 minutes then remove from heat then season to taste with salt & pepper then stir in chopped cilantro to serve chicken breast place chicken breast on a dinner plate then spoon sauce over chicken then serve with rice, or potatoes, vegetables.

SAUTE CHICKEN THIGHS
WITH CRAB, CONCH AND CHILI PEPPERS

Makes 6 servings

Ingredients:
- 1   1 lb can jumbo lump crab meat
- 1   1 lb can conch meat beaten to tenderize it, slice thin
- 3   lbs boneless chicken thighs cleaned, medium diced
- 3   medium jalapeno chili peppers, seeded and diced
- 3   medium Serrano Chile peppers, seeded and diced
- 3   medium Anaheim Chile pepper, seeded and diced
- 3   medium red and green bell peppers, seeded and diced
- 1 ½   cups all-purpose flour seasoned, for dredging chicken
- ⅓   cup olive oil
- 3   tablespoons fresh garlic cloves, finely chopped
- 2   tablespoons fresh ginger, finely chopped
- 2 ½   cups new groove chicken stock, see recipe
- 3 ½   tablespoons smoked chipotle paste
- 5   medium Roma tomatoes, medium diced
- 1   medium Vidalia onion peeled, medium diced
- 1   medium ripe mango peeled, medium diced
- 4   tablespoons sweet cream butter
- ⅓   cup absolut peppar vodka
- ⅓   cup Cruzan mango rum
- ⅓   cup Cruzan citrus rum
-       New groove house seasoning blend, to taste
- 1   bunch fresh tarragon chopped, for garnish
- 1   1 lb box penne pasta, cooked
- 2   cups white rice, cooked

Procedure:

In a large mixing bowl add 1 1/2 cups flour seasoned with new groove house seasoning blend then dredge your chicken thighs in flour and shake off any excess flour

And set aside then in a large 14 inch sauté pan over medium heat add your olive oil then add your chicken and cook for 6 minutes then remove chicken from sauté pan

Then put aside and then in the same large sauté pan over medium heat add your roma tomatoes, garlic, ginger, onion, bell peppers, Chile peppers then stir cook for 6 minutes

Then add your chicken, conch meat, jumbo lump crab meat, chicken stock, citrus rum, mango rum, peppar vodka then stir then simmer for 25 minutes over low heat

Then season to taste with new groove house seasoning blend then stir in diced mango and sweet cream butter then remove heat. To serve place rice or pasta on

Dinner plates then spoon sauté mixture over rice or pasta then garnish with chopped tarragon. Then serve.

NEW GROOVE MIAMI STYLE CITRUS CHICKEN

Makes 6 servings

Ingredients:

- 6   6 oz boneless breast of chicken seasoned with, new groove house seasoning
- 3   tablespoons fresh ginger, finely chopped
- 2   tablespoons fresh garlic, finely chopped
-      Zest and segments from 2 limes, diced
-      Zest and segments from 2 blood oranges, diced
- ¼   cup olive oil
- 3   tablespoons sweet cream butter
- ½   cup coconut flakes, lightly toasted
- ½   cup macadamia nut slightly toasted, coarsely ground
- 1   cup chicken stock, see recipe
- ⅓   cup Cruzan Citrus Rum
- ⅓   cup Smirnoff Vanilla Vodka
- 4   Jalapeño chilies, seeded and diced
- 4   Anaheim chilies, seeded and diced
- 2   teaspoons nutmeg
- 2   teaspoons allspice
-      Season to taste with new groove house seasoning

Procedure:

In a large saute pan over medium heat then add your oil and butter. Then add garlic and ginger then stir and saute for 2 minutes then add chicken breast with a 1/3 cup of chicken then stock cook for 8 minutes then add the rest of your chicken stock one tablespoon of each lime and orange zest, lime and orange segments jalapeno and Anaheim chilies, coconut flakes, macadamia nuts, nutmeg allspice, vanilla rum citrus rum. Then stir and cook for 4 to 5 minutes then reduce heat to low. Then cover and simmer for an additional 5 minutes then season to taste with New Groove House seasoning. Then remove chicken from saute pan and place on plates. Then pour sauce on top and then garnish with lime and orange zest, toasted crushed macadamia nuts then serve.

CARIBBEAN PORK MEDALLIONS WITH COCONUT AND CHILI PEPPERS

Makes 5 servings

Ingredients:

2	pounds pork tenderloin, cleaned, seasoned, cut ½" thick
⅓	cup olive oil
2	cups coconut milk
2	cups coconut flakes, toasted
4	fresh shallots, finely chopped
3	tablespoons garlic cloves, finely chopped
3	tablespoons ginger, finely chopped
1	teaspoon ground allspice
1	tablespoon ground cinnamon
1	tablespoon ground nutmeg
3	tablespoons Thai basil, chopped
3	tablespoons fresh cilantro, chopped
3	fresh Habanero Chile peppers, seeded and chopped
3	fresh Jalapeño Chile peppers, seeded and chopped
3	fresh Thai Chile peppers, seeded and chopped
⅓	cup Absolut Mandarin Vodka
⅓	cup Absolut Vodka
⅓	cup Jose Cuervo Tequila
⅓	cup Bacardi Coconut Rum
2	11 oz cans mandarin oranges in juice, well drained
1 ¼	cups walnuts, black, chopped and toasted
	New groove house seasoning or salt and pepper to taste

Procedure:

First clean and cut pork tenderloin into 1/2" thick medallions. Season with new groove house seasoning in a large 8 qt Dutch oven over medium high heat, add olive oil. Add pork medallions and cook for 4 minutes per side then transfer to a platter to keep warm. Add shallots, garlic, ginger, habanero chili peppers, jalapeño Chile peppers, Thai Chile peppers, black walnuts, allspice, cinnamon and nutmeg. Stir and cook for 4 minutes then lower heat to medium. Add coconut milk, coconut flakes, mandarin oranges, coconut rum, tequila, Absolut mandarin vodka. Stir and simmer for 13 minutes then remove from heat. Stir in Thai basil and cilantro. Season to taste with new groove house seasoning then serve over top pork medallions. Garnish with fresh chopped chives.

WILD MUSHROOMS AND GARLIC OVER SAUTED PORK MEDALLIONS

Makes 5 servings

Ingredients:
- 3 pounds pork tenderloin cleaned seasoned, cut ½" thick
- ⅓ cup olive oil
- 2 14 oz cans artichoke hearts, sliced
- 1 ½ cups shitake mushrooms, stems removed sliced
- 1 ½ cups chanterelle mushrooms, stems removed sliced
- 1 cup hazelnuts, toasted
- 3 tablespoons ginger, finely chopped
- 4 fresh red jalapeño chili peppers, seeded and chopped
- 5-6 fresh garlic cloves, finely chopped
- ⅓ cup Grand Marnier
- ⅓ cup Bacardi Rum
- New groove fusion house seasoning or salt and pepper to taste
- 1 bunch fresh lemon basil chopped for garnish

Procedure:

First cleaned and cut pork tenderloin into ½" thick medallions. Season with new groove fusion house seasoning or salt pepper. In a large sauté pan over medium high heat, add olive oil and pork medallions. Sauté for 4 minutes per side then transfer pork to a platter. Keep warm. Add mushrooms, ginger, garlic, hazelnuts, red jalapeño chili pepper, artichokes bottoms, rum and Grand Marnier. Sauté for 8 minutes. Season to taste with new groove fusion house seasoning or salt and pepper. Serve spooned over pork medallions. Garnish with fresh chopped lemon basil. Serve with vegetables and mashed potatoes.

GRILLED PORK MEDALLIONS WITH GLAZED APPLES AND PEARS

Makes 6 servings

Ingredients:

1	5 pound pork tenderloin cleaned cut into 1" inch, medallions then grilled

Sauce for pork

2	sticks sweet cream butter, softened
1 ¼	cup garlic cloves, chopped
3	tablespoons fresh ginger, chopped
3	tablespoons dry mustard
3	fresh Thai Chilie peppers, seeded and chopped
½	cup light brown sugar
3	medium Granny Smith apples cored, peeled, cut into wedges
3	medium pears cored, peeled, cut into wedges
1	cup flour, all-purpose
1 ½	cups apple cider, add to stock
1 ½	cups French apple brandy (calvados), add to stock
1 ½	cups absolut pear vodka, add to stock
2	quarts chicken stock or water, add to stock
	New groove grill blends 1, season to taste

Procedure:

First clean and cut pork tenderloin into one inch round medallions then season medallions with salt & pepper then grill pork medallions until done then place pork medallions on a large platter keep warm. Then in a large 8 qt Dutch oven over medium high heat add butter, garlic, ginger, Thai Chilie peppers stir cook for 3 minutes then add apple wedges, pear wedges dry mustard, brown sugar, stir cook for 5 minutes then stir in flour cook for 3 minutes then add chicken stock or water, apple cider, apple brandy, pear vodka stir bring to a boil

Let sauce boil until reduced to sauce consistency then remove from heat season to taste with salt & pepper. Then pour sauce over grilled pork medallions then serve.

FLAVORFUL GRILLED PORK MEDALLIONS

WITH A SPICY ROASTED YELLOW PEPPER SAUCE WITH TEQUILA, PEPPAR VODKA AND CHAMPAGNE

Makes 4 servings

Ingredients:
- 1 large pork tenderloin cut ½ inch thick, cleaned
- ⅓ cup vegetable oil, brush on pork
- 3 tablespoons kosher salt, season pork
- 3 tablespoons ground black pepper, season pork

For roasted yellow pepper sauce
- 10 medium yellow bell peppers, roasted and peeled
- ⅓ cup vegetable oil
- ⅓ cup Champagne
- ½ cup Absolut peppar vodka
- ⅓ cup Jose Cuervo tequila
- 5 small yellow chili peppers, roasted and peeled
- 1 teaspoon cayenne pepper
- 3 tablespoons lemon zest
- New groove grill blends II, season to taste
- ⅓ cup vegetable oil, brush on peppers

Procedure:

First clean pork tenderloin then cut into ½ inch thick medallions then brush medallions with oil then season with salt & pepper then grill pork medallions

For about 3 minutes per side then remove medallions from grill place on a platter keep warm. Then pre heat at 400°F then rub yellow bell peppers, yellow chili peppers with vegetable oil then place peppers on a large baking sheet then roasted peppers at 400°F for 15 to 20 minutes Then remove peppers from oven then place peppers

In a plastic bag or a paper bag for 10 minutes then peel and seed peppers then place peppers in a large food processor with vegetable oil champagne, peppar vodka

Tequila, cayenne pepper, lemon zest then process until smooth season to taste with kosher salt. Then serve sauce with grilled pork medallions.

ROAST PORK TENDERLOIN
WITH FRESH HERBS NEW GROOVE STYLE

Makes 6 servings

Ingredients:

- 5 pound pork tenderloin cleaned N butterflied then season salt N pepper
- ¼ pound prosciutto ham, sliced thin
- 3 cups fresh bread crumbs
- ¼ cup garlic cloves, finely chopped
- 4 tablespoons fresh ginger, finely chopped
- 1 cup pine nuts, toasted
- 1 bunch fresh rosemary, finely chopped
- 1 bunch fresh basil, finely chopped
- 1 bunch fresh oregano, finely chopped
- 1 bunch fresh thyme, finely chopped
- 1 bunch fresh sage, finely chopped
- 1 bunch fresh marjoram, finely chopped
- 1 bunch fresh tarragon, finely chopped
- 1 cup olive oil, to brush top
- Salt and pepper, to season to taste

Procedure:

First pre-heat oven at 325°F then clean and butterflied then season pork tenderloin with salt & pepper then in a large bowl add bread crumbs, garlic, ginger, pine nuts

All the fresh chopped herbs salt & pepper to taste then layer prosciutto ham then top with bread crumb mixture then fold over pork tenderloin place on a large baking sheet seam side down brush with olive oil bake at 325°F for about 30 to 35 minutes then remove from oven let pork rest for 10 minutes then slice and serve With vegetables mashed or roasted potatoes

SAUTED PORK MEDALLIONS

WITH PLUM TOMATOES, ITALIAN HOT PEPPERS, RED ONIONS, BLACK OLIVES LACED WITH COGNAC, BLACK RUM AND CHAMPAGNE

Makes 6 servings

Ingredients:

- 1 large pork tenderloin clean & cut season s&p, pound ¼ inch thick
- 1 cup black pitted olives, drained
- 3 medium Italian hot peppers, seeded slice thin
- 1 medium red onion, sliced thin
- 6 medium plum tomatoes, diced
- 3 cups chicken stock
- 1 cup Gosling black seal rum
- 1 cup Champagne
- 2 cups Hennessey cognac
- 1 cup water, mix together
- ⅓ cup arrowroot powder, mix together
- 1 cup vegetable oil

    New Groove House Seasoning, season to taste

Procedure:

First clean and cut pork tenderloin then pound pork medallions until thin then season with salt & pepper then in a large bowl add flour then dredge pork medallions in flour shaking off excess flour then in a large 8 qt Dutch oven over medium high heat add oil then pork medallions cook for 4 minutes per side then remove pork medallions place on a large platter keep warm. Then wipe out Dutch oven then in the same Dutch oven over medium heat add tomatoes, black olives hot peppers, onions cook for 3 minutes then add chicken stock black rum, champagne, cognac bring to a boil then add arrowroot mixed with water cook until sauce starts to thicken then reduce heat simmer for 7 minutes then remove from heat season to taste with salt & pepper. Then pour sauce over pork medallions serve with your favorite side dishes

NEW GROOVE FUSION PORK CORDON BLEU
WITH A LEMON RUM CAPER SAUCE

Makes 6 servings

Ingredients:

1	5 pound pork tenderloin cleaned & butter filed, seasoned with s&p
6	cups fresh bread crumbs
¼	pound provolone cheese, sliced thin
¼	pound prosciutto, sliced thin
4	cups flour, all-purpose
3	cups milk, mix together
5	jumbo eggs, mix together
1	small jar capers
½	cup water, mix together
5	tablespoons arrowroot powder, mix together
3 ½	cups chicken stock
½	cup lemon juice, bottled
1	cup Bacardi limon rum
1 ½	cups Bacardi gold rum
	Salt and pepper, to taste

Procedure:

First clean and butter filed pork tenderloin then season pork tenderloin with salt & pepper then layer in prosciutto ham, provolone cheese then folds tenderloin

Into a jelly roll seam side down then dredge pork tenderloin in flour, then in egg & milk mixture, then in breadcrumbs then place pork tenderloin on a large baking sheet bake

at 350*F for about 35 to 40 minutes then remove pork tenderloin from oven let rest for 10 minutes before slicing. Then in a large 4 qt sauce pan over high heat add chicken stock

Lemon juice, gold rum, limon rum, capers bring to a boil then add arrowroot mix with water stir reduce heat cook until sauce starts to thicken remove from heat season to taste with salt & pepper. Serve with sliced pork tenderloin. And your favorite side dishes

SPICY VEAL SALTIMBOCCA
WITH A PLUM TOMATO CHAMPAGNE RUM SAUCE

Makes 6 servings

Ingredients:
- 3 pounds veal cutlets, pound ¼ inch thick
- 3 ½ cups flour, all-purpose
- 6 jumbo eggs, beaten
- 6 cups fresh bread crumbs
- 2 ½ cups milk, add to eggs
- ⅓ pound prosciutto ham, sliced thin
- 5 small fresh Thai Chile peppers, seeded and chopped
- 2 tablespoons crushed red pepper flakes
- 2 tablespoons fresh oregano, chopped
- 2 tablespoons fresh basil, chopped
- 2 tablespoons fresh sage, chopped
- ⅓ pound provolone cheese, sliced thin
- 3 cups veal stock or chicken stock
- 8 medium plum tomatoes, diced
- 1 cup olive oil
- 2 cups Champagne
- 2 cups Bacardi gold rum
- 1 cup water, mix together
- ⅓ cup cornstarch, mix together
- Salt and Pepper, to taste

Procedure:

First pre heat oven at 350°F then in a large bowl add flour then another large bowl add milk and eggs then in another bowl add your bread crumbs, Thai Chile peppers

Red pepper flakes, oregano, basil, sage, salt & pepper to taste mix well. Then dredge your veal cutlets in flour, then in egg mixture then in seasoned bread crumbs

Then in a large 8 qt Dutch oven over medium high heat add olive oil then brown your veal cutlets on both sides then place your browned veal cutlets on a large baking sheet then top veal with prosciutto ham then provolone cheese then place baking sheet in oven bake at 350°F for 15 minutes then remove veal from oven then place veal on a large

Oval platters keep warm. Then for sauce in large 4 qt sauce pan over medium high heat add chicken stock or veal stock, diced plum tomatoes, champagne, rum bring to a boil then add cornstarch mixed with water cook until sauce starts to thicken then lower heat simmer for 5 minutes then remove from heat season to taste with salt & pepper.

Then spoon sauce over veal cutlets then serve.

VEAL MEDALIONS
WITH APPLES, DATES, PINE NUTS AND FRENCH APPLE BRANDY

Makes 6 servings

Ingredients:

- 3 pounds veal cutlets, pound ¼ inch thick
- 3 cups flour, all-purpose
- 3 cups dates
- 6 medium Granny Smith apples, peeled and sliced
- 1 cup pine nuts, toasted
- 4 cups veal stock or chicken stock
- 1 cup light brown sugar
- 1 ¼ cups French apple brandy (calvados)
- 1 ¼ cups Hennessy Cognac
- 1 cup olive oil
- 1 bunch fresh cilantro, chopped
- 1 ½ cups water, mix together
- ½ cup cornstarch, mix together
- Salt and pepper, to taste
- 2 sticks sweet cream butter, softened

Procedure:

First pound out veal cutlets then season veal cutlets with salt & pepper than in a large bowl add flour then dredge veal cutlets in flour shake off excess flour then in a large 8 qt Dutch oven over medium high heat add olive oil then add veal cutlets brown veal on both sides then transfer veal cutlets to a large platter keep warm then wipe out Dutch oven then add butter to Dutch oven over medium high heat add sliced apples, brown sugar, dates, pine nuts stir cook for 5 minutes then add veal stock or chicken stock, apple brandy cognac stir bring sauce to a boil then add cornstarch mixed with water cook until sauce starts to thicken then reduce heat simmer for 15 minutes then stir in cilantro

Then remove from heat season to taste with salt & pepper. Spoon sauces over veal cutlets then serve

VEAL MEDALIONS
WITH BLACK OLIVES, TOMATOES, AND ARTICHOKES

Makes 6 servings

Ingredients:

- 3 pounds veal cutlets season with salt & pepper, pound ¼ inch thick
- 3 cups flour, all-purpose
- 1 cup black pitted olives
- 2 cups artichoke bottoms, sliced
- 2 cups plum tomatoes, diced
- 3 tablespoons fresh garlic, finely chopped
- 1 ½ cups veal stock or chicken stock
- 1 tablespoon fresh finger, finely chopped
- 1 cup olive oil
- 1 cup Hennessy Cognac
- 1 cup Champagne
- Salt and Pepper, to taste

Procedure:

First pound out veal cutlets then season veal cutlets with salt & pepper then in a large bowl add your flour then dredge veal cutlets in flour shake off excess flour

Then in a large 8 qt Dutch oven over medium high heat add olive oil then veal brown on both sides then transfers veal cutlets to a large platter keep warm. Then lower heat to medium

Then add black olives, ginger, garlic, tomatoes, artichoke bottoms, veal stock or chicken stock, champagne, cognac stir simmer for 20 minutes then stir in basil then season

To taste with salt & pepper then remove from heat. Serve sauce with veal. Medallions

CHEF SIGNATURE RECIPE
SAUTE VEAL CUTLET'S

WITH WILD MUSHROOMS, TARRAGON, OREGANO, CHAMPAGNE AND RUM

Makes 6 servings

Ingredients:

- 3 pounds veal cutlets seasoned with salt & pepper, pound ¼ inch thick
- 3 cups flour, all-purpose
- 4 cups wild mushrooms, sliced
- ¼ cup fresh tarragon, chopped
- ¼ cup fresh oregano, chopped
- 3 ½ cups veal stock or chicken stock
- 1 cup Champagne
- 1 cup Bacardi dark rum
- 1 cup Cruzan vanilla rum
- 1 cup olive oil
- Salt and Pepper, to taste
- 2 sticks sweet cream butter, softened

Procedure:

First pound out veal cutlets then season veal cutlets with salt & pepper then in a large bowl add flour then dredge veal cutlets in flour shaking off excess flour

Then in a large 8 qt Dutch oven over medium high heat add olive oil then veal cutlets brown on both sides transfer veal cutlets to a large platter keep warm then add butter to Dutch oven then add wild mushrooms cook for 3 minutes then add veal stock or chicken stock, rum, dark rum, vanilla rum, champagne simmer for 21 minutes then stir in Tarragon, oregano season to taste with salt & pepper then remove from heat serve sauce with veal cutlets

BREADED VEAL CUTLETS
WITH A CHAMPAGNE, TARRAGON CREAM SAUCE

Makes 5 servings

Ingredients:
- 3 pounds veal cutlets, pound ¼ inch thick
- Salt and pepper, season veal
- 2 ½ cups all-purpose flour
- 4 jumbo eggs, add to milk
- 2 cups milk, add to eggs
- 9 cups fresh bread crumbs, mix together
- 2 tablespoons fresh cilantro, mix together
- 2 tablespoons fresh basil, mix together
- 2 tablespoons fresh oregano, mix together
- 2 tablespoons fresh thyme, mix together
- 2 cups Parmesan cheese, mix together

For making roux
- 1 ½ cups all-purpose flour, add to butter
- 1 ½ sticks sweet cream butter

For champagne tarragon cream sauce
- 2 ½ cups milk
- 2 ½ cups heavy cream
- 2 cups Champagne
- ¼ cup fresh tarragon, chopped
- Salt and white pepper, to taste
- 1 cup Canola oil, to cook veal

Procedure:

First pound your veal cutlets then season with salt & pepper then put aside then in a large mixing bowl add flour, then in another large mixing bowl add eggs and milk beat until blended then put aside then in another large mixing bowl add bread crumbs, cilantro, basil, oregano, thyme, parmesan cheese stir to blend then dredge veal cutlets in flour shaking off excess flour then dredge in egg & milk mixture then in bread crumbs then in a large 8 qt Dutch oven over medium high heat add canola oil then breaded veal cutlets cook for about 4 minutes per side then transfer veal cutlets to a large serving platter keep warm. Then in a large 4 qt sauce pan over medium heat add butter, flour stir cook for 3 minutes to make Roux then add milk, heavy cream whisk until smooth cook until sauce starts to thicken then strain sauce then add sauce back to the sauce pan then add tarragon, champagne stir

Then simmer for 4 minutes then remove from heat season to taste with salt & white pepper. Spoon sauce over veal cutlets.

MARINADE GRILLED VEAL CHOPS AND LIME CITRUS SAUCE

Makes 5 servings

Ingredients:
5   8 oz veal chops, marinated

Marinade for veal chops:
1 ½   cups veal stock, see recipe
1   cup fresh lime juice
⅓   cup teriyaki sauce
2   tablespoons crushed red pepper
2   tablespoons New Groove Italian-Mediterranean Seasoning
3   tablespoons garlic cloves, chopped
3   tablespoons ginger, chopped
½   cup canola oil

For lime citrus sauce:
2   cups veal stock, see recipe
1 ⅓   cups fresh lime juice
3   tablespoons lime zest, minced
2   tablespoons orange zest, minced
3   tablespoons fresh cilantro, chopped for garnish
3   blood oranges peeled and sectioned
1 ⅓   cups Cabernet Sauvignon
1 ⅓   cups Bacardi Dark Rum
⅓   cup cornstarch
1   cup water
    Salt and pepper, to taste
4   tablespoons orange zest for garnish

Procedure:

Place veal chops in a large 4 qt baking dish. Combine with ginger, shallots, garlic, crushed red pepper, teriyaki sauce, lime juice and veal stock in a large bowl and stir. Pour over veal chops then marinade for 2 to 4 hours. Grill basting veal chops with marinade. In a large 4 qt sauce pan over medium high heat add veal stock, lime juice, lime zest, orange zest, cabernet sauvignon and rum. Stir and bring sauce to a boil. In a small bowl combine cornstarch and water. Add to sauce and cook until sauce starts to thicken. Stir in blood orange sections and cilantro. Season to taste with salt and pepper. Remove sauce from heat. Serve with grilled veal chops. Garnish with orange zest and chopped cilantro.

STUFFED VEAL CHOP WITH A CRANBERRY PEAR SAUCE

Makes 5 servings

Ingredients:

- 5   12 oz veal chop cut a silt to make a pocket, seasoned
- ⅓   cup Canola oil

Stuffing for veal chops:

- 4   cups foccaccia bread crumbs
- ½   pound Italian sausage, cooked and crumbled
- 4   jumbo eggs
- 2   tablespoons fresh sage, chopped
- 2   tablespoons Thai basil, chopped
- 2   tablespoons fresh rosemary, chopped
- 1   cup fresh dates, chopped
- 1   cup pine nuts, toasted
- 1   cup hazelnuts, toasted
- 1   cup dried cranberries
- 1   pound jumbo lump crab meat
- ¼   cup Hennessy Cognac optional
- ¼   cup Cruzan Vanilla Rum optional

    Season with "New Groove House Seasoning or salt and pepper

- 1   bunch fresh rosemary chopped for garnish
- 1   bunch fresh sage chopped for garnish

For cranberry pear sauce:

- 3 cups fusion veal stock
- 2 cups dried cranberries
- 6 fresh Bartlett pears, peeled and sliced
- 1 cup Smirnoff craneberry Apple Vodka
- 1 cup Absolut Pear Vodka
- ⅓ cup Cruzan Dark Rum
- ½ cup cornstarch, mixed with water
- 1 cup water
- Salt and pepper, to taste

Procedure:

First make a pocket on the side of the veal chop. Season veal chops with new groove house seasoning then put aside. In large mixing bowl combine bread crumbs, crab meat, lobster meat, dates, cranberries, rosemary, Thai basil, sage, eggs, pine nuts, hazelnuts, Italian sausage, cognac and vanilla rum. Mix well. Season to taste with "new groove house seasoning" or salt and pepper. Stuff veal chops. In a large sauté pan over high heat add canola oil then veal chops. Cook for 2 minutes per side then transfer veal chops to a non-stick baking sheet. Place in oven and bake at 350°F for 15 minutes. Keep warm. In a 4 qt sauce pan over medium high heat add veal stock, dried cranberries, sliced pears, gold rum, cranberry vodka and pear vodka. Bring to a boil. In small bowl combine cornstarch and water. Add to sauce and cook until sauce starts to thicken. Reduce heat and simmer for 20 minutes. Season to taste with new groove house seasoning or salt and pepper. Then serve sauce with stuffed veal chops. Garnish with fresh chopped sage and rosemary.

Fish & Seafood...

Always a favorite I bring you the very best the oceans and seas have. To offer from fresh lobster and jumbo lump crab meat from. The waters of maine, south Africa to fresh prawns and scallops from Maryland. To the gulf of Mexico and a wide / vast variety of fish from the Atlantic and pacific oceans. My signature seafood dishes showcase what. My style of fusion is all like my other dishes. I use only top quality choice fresh seafood and fish then. I marry them with common to exotic ingredients herbs, spices, liqueurs and flavorings to create a fusion inspired culinary masterpiece.

SLICKRICK'S SALMON MARSALA OVER RICE

Ingredients:
- 5   8 oz Salmon Filet skin removed
- ½   cup canola oil for cooking salmon
- 7   slices of Duck bacon diced
- 1   medium size leek sliced thin
- 1   Bulb of fresh garlic peeled and chopped
- 4   Tablespoon Tomato paste
- 2   cups wild mushroom sliced
- ½   cup pinenuts
- 1   bunch fresh flat leaf parsley chopped
- 1   bunch fresh chives sliced thin for garnish
- 2   cups seafood stock
- 2   cups Bacardi Black rum
- 3 ¼   cups Marsala Wine
-       Kosher salt and coarse ground black pepper to taste
- 2   cups of wild rice blend cooked

Procedure:

First in a large 8 quart dutch oven over medium high heat add your canola oil then add your salmon filets cook for 3 minutes per side then remove salmon filets place on a large platter keep warm then in the same Dutch oven over medium high heat add your Duck bacon stir cook for 6 minutes then remove duck bacon

Put aside then add your garlic, leeks, pinenuts, wild mushrooms stir cook for 4 minutes then add your duck bacon parsley, seafood stock, black rum, Marsala wine, tomato paste stir then bring to simmer. Simmer for 4 minutes then remove from heat then season to taste with Kosher salt and coarse ground black pepper. To serve place your cooked wild rice blend on a Dinner plate then place Salmon on top then ladel Marsala sauce over salmon then garnish with fresh chives.

Serves 5 people

BLACKENED CHILEAN SEA BASS FILETS
WITH A CITRUS BOURBON SAUCE

Makes 2 servings

Ingredients:
- 2   8 oz Chilean sea bass filets, cleaned

Recipe for blacking spice
- ¼ cup dried parsley, mix together
- ¼ cup dried thyme, mix together
- 1 cup paprika, mix together
- ¼ cup cayenne pepper, mix together
- ¼ cup salt, mix together
- ¼ cup ground black pepper, mix together
- ¼ cup ground white pepper, mix together
- ¼ cup chili powder, mix together
- ¼ cup cumin, mix together
- ¼ cup curry powder, mix together
- ¼ ground coriander, mix together
- ¼ cup vegetable oil to make paste, add to spice
- ¼ cup peanut oil, to cook fish

Recipe for citrus bourbon sauce
- 1 ⅓ cups water, mix together
- ¼ cup lime juice, mix together
- ¼ cup orange juice, mix together
- ¼ cup lemon juice, mix together
- 1 tablespoon lime zest, mix together
- 1 tablespoon orange zest, mix together

1	tablespoon lemon zest, mix together
⅓	cup light brown sugar, mix together
1	cup knob creek bourbon mix together
½	cup water, add to
⅓	cup cornstarch, mix with water
	Salt and white pepper, to taste

Procedure:

First in a large mixing bowl combine parsley, thyme, white pepper, black pepper, salt, paprika, cayenne pepper, chili powder, cumin, coriander, curry powder then mix well until blended then in a medium size mixing bowl add 1 cup of blackening spice and 1/3 cup vegetable oil to make paste then add fish one at a time turn to coat

Then in a medium sauté pan over medium high heat add peanut oil then add sea bass filets cook for 3 to 4 minutes per side then transfer blackened sea bass to a medium platter

Keep warm. Then in a large 4 qt sauce pan over medium heat add water, lime juice, orange juice, lemon juice, lemon zest, orange zest, lime zest, bourbon, and brown sugar.

Then stir then bring sauce to a boil then add cornstarch mixed with water cook until sauce starts to thicken then remove from heat season to taste with salt & white pepper.

Then drizzle sauce over blackened sea bass. Serve with steam vegetables and rice pilaf

THREE GREEN PASTA WITH SCALLOPS, SEA BASS, LOBSTER, AND ROCK SHRIMP

Makes 5 servings

Ingredients:

- 1 bunch fresh asparagus trimmed blanched, cut 1 ½ inches
- 1 lb package Penne, Pappardelle, Fettuccine or Spaghetti, linguine
- ½ pound fresh green beans trimmed blanched, cut 1 ½ inches
- 1 package frozen green peas, blanched
- 2 pounds dry sack scallops
- 2 pounds lobster tail meat, sliced
- 2 pounds sea bass fillets, sliced
- 2 pounds rock shrimp
- 1 ¼ cups whole almonds, toasted
- 1 bunch Thai basil, sliced thin
- 1 bunch cinnamon basil, sliced thin
- 1 bunch lemon thyme
- 1 tablespoon crush red pepper flakes
- ½ cup Absolut Citron Vodka
- ½ cup Cruzan vanilla rum
- 1 ½ cups pesto sauce
- 1 ¼ cups heavy cream
- ¼ cup orange juice
- ½ cup safflower oil
- Salt and Pepper, to taste

Procedure:

First bring a large 8 qt Dutch oven of salted water to a boil add asparagus and green beans cook for about 3 minutes then drain and rinse under cold water to stop cooking

Then in the same Dutch oven cook your pasta then drain the pasta then in the same Dutch oven over medium high heat adds safflower oil then lobster meat, rock shrimp, sea bass, scallops

Almonds, Thai basil, cinnamon basil, lemon thyme, crushed red pepper flakes, Citron Vodka, vanilla rum. Cook for about 5 minutes then add green beans, green peas, and asparagus then stir then lower heat then add pesto sauce, heavy cream, orange juice stir simmer for 3 minutes then remove from heat then season to taste with salt & pepper then place your cooked pasta on a large oval platter then pour seafood mixture over pasta then toss and serve..

GRILLED HALIBUT FILETS WITH A SPICY MAPLE RUM SAUCE

Makes 6 servings

Ingredients:
- 6 — 1" thick cut halibut filets season with salt & pepper, grilled
- ⅓ cup vegetable oil, drizzle over fish
- Salt and Pepper, to season fish

Recipe for spicy maple rum sauce
- 1 ⅓ cups water, mix together
- ⅔ cup orange juice, mix together
- ⅓ cup Don Q 151 rum
- ⅓ cup Bacardi dark rum mix together
- 1 ½ cups maple syrup, mix together
- 4 fresh Thai Chile peppers, mix together
- 2 fresh red jalapeno chili peppers, mix together
- 3 tablespoons fresh cilantro, add to sauce
- ½ cup water, add to
- ¼ cup cornstarch, mix together
- Salt and Pepper, to taste

Procedure:

First season halibut filets with salt & pepper then drizzle with vegetable oil then grill fish over medium high heat for about 4 minutes per side

Then transfer fish to a large platter keep warm then in a large 4 qt sauce pan over medium high heat add water, orange juice, 151 rum dark rum, maple syrup

Thai Chile peppers, red jalapeno chili peppers stir then bring sauce to a boil then add cornstarch mixed with water then cook until sauce starts to thicken then remove

From heat stir in cilantro then season to taste with salt & pepper. Serve sauce with the grilled fish. Along with corn on the cob and a toss salad.

NEW GROOVE FUSZION PAPPARDELLE SUGO POMOBORO D'MARI

Ingredients:

- 1 lb package Pappardelle Pasta cooked
- 1 cup pinenuts
- 10 Fresh garlic cloves Roasted finely chopped
- 1 bunch fresh Basil Chopped
- 1 bunch fresh Flat leaf Parsley chopped
- 1 bunch fresh Oregano chopped
- 5 fresh Italian Hot peppers seeded and sliced
- 2 cups frozen sweet peas
- 1 medium size Vidalia onion peeled and small diced
- 1 lb package of Chorizo sausage sliced
- 1 lb can Jumbo Lump crab meat
- 1 lb package Calamari Rings with tentacles chopped
- 1 ½ lbs package whole lobster meat tail and claws
- 1 28 oz can crushed tomatoes
- 1 cup Olive oil
- 2 cups Chicken stock or seafood stock
- 1 ½ cups White Wine
- 1 ½ cups Merlot Wine
- 2 cups fresh grated parmesan cheese

Kosher salt and coarse ground black pepper to taste

Procedure:

In large 8 quart dutch oven over medium heat add your olive oil, onions, peppers, sausage, garlic stir and cook for 4 minutes then add, your chicken stock or seafood stock, pinenuts, peas, crushed tomatoes, white wine cover and simmer for 15 minutes, then add your Merlot Wine.

Calamari rings with chopped tentacles whole sliced lobster meat Jumbo lump crab meat, some chopped Basil, Parsley, Oregano Cover simmer for another 10 minutes, then season to taste with kosher salt and coarse ground black pepper then remove from heat then cook your Pappardelle pasta then drain pasta then toss with Olive oil then place pasta in a large oval dish then pour sauce over pasta toss then top with parmesan cheese, parsley, Oregano, Basil then serve.

NEW GROOVE STYLE SHRIMP SCAMPI

Makes 6 servings

Ingredients:

- 3 pounds 16/20 jumbo shrimp, SHELLED AND CLEANED
- 2 pounds jumbo lump crab meat
- 4 tablespoons garlic cloves, chopped
- 2 tablespoons fresh lemon thyme
- 1 bunch fresh green onions, sliced thin
- 2 tablespoons fresh chervil, chopped
- 3 tablespoons fresh cilantro, chopped
- 2 teaspoons fresh lime zest, use a zestier
- 3 fresh Thai chili peppers, seeded and chopped
- 1 cup olive oil
- 2 cups Champagne
- ½ cup Absolut citron Vodka
- ½ cup myers's rum original dark Jamaican rum
- ⅓ cup Jose Cuervo gold tequila
- New groove house seasoning or kosher salt, to taste
- 1 package pasta, cooked and drained
- 2 cups white rice, cooked

Procedure:

In a large 8 qt Dutch oven over medium heat add olive oil, garlic, Thai chili pepper, lemon thyme, lime zest, champagne, Citron vodka, gold tequila, dark rum. Bring to a simmer then add shrimp, jumbo lump crab meat. Stir cook for about 5 minutes or until shrimp turn pink then stir in Green onions chervil, cilantro. Season to taste with new Groove House Seasoning Blend or kosher salt remove from heat. Then serve with rice or pasta.

NEW GROOVE FISH H' RAIMI

Makes 8 servings

Ingredients:

1	1 cup olive oil
⅓	cup chopped garlic
¼	cup lime juice
2	tablespoons chili powder
3	tablespoons kosher salt
1 ¼	tablespoons black pepper
5	Serrano chili peppers, seeded and chopped
2 ½	tablespoons tomato paste
1 ¼	cups Hennessey cognac
2	lbs of each grouper, sea bass, halibut, cut into ¾ thick pieces
1 ¼	cups Champagne
1 ¼	cups water
1	cup bread crumbs
½	cup chives, chopped, garnish
1	cup pine nuts, toasted

Procedure:

First pre-heat oven to 350°F place pine nuts on cookie tray cook for about 3 to 4 minutes until lightly toasted then in a large 10 qt Dutch oven

Over medium high heat add oil garlic sauté for 3 minutes then add lime juice, chili powder, salt, black pepper, Serrano chili peppers, cognac, and champagne tomato paste stir add fish, water bring to a boil then reduce heat to low simmer for 20 minutes remove from heat stir in bread crumbs pine nuts. Then transfer fish to large serving platter then garnish

With fresh chives then serve with steam vegetables and rice pilaf

CURRIED LOBSTER SHRIMP PILAU FUSION STYLE

Makes 8 servings

Ingredients:

- 2 pounds jumbo 16/20 shrimp, SHELLED AND CLEANED
- 2 pounds canned lobster meat
- ⅓ cup lime juice
- ⅓ cup Bacardi coconut rum
- ⅓ cup French brandy
- ⅓ cup Myers's dark rum
- 4 ¼ cups coconut milk, add to rice
- ⅓ cup safflower oil
- 1 large Vidalia onion, finely chopped
- 3 tablespoons curry powder
- 3 tablespoons garlic cloves
- 4 fresh Thai Chile peppers, seeded and minced
- 3 fresh jalapeno Chile peppers, seeded and minced
- 2 ⅓ cups long-grain white rice
- Salt and Pepper, to taste
- 1 bunch flat leaf parsley chopped, garnish

Procedure:

In a large mixing bowl add your cleaned shrimp and lobster meat then add lime juice, coconut rum, Myers's dark rum, French brandy then set aside then in a large 8 quart Dutch oven over medium heat add safflower oil, onion, Jalapeno Chile peppers, Thai Chile peppers, garlic, curry powder stir cook for 3 minutes then add rice stir well to coat rice then pour in coconut milk stir then cover and cook over low heat for about 20 minutes stir occasionally add more liquid if necessary then add shrimp & lobster meat and marinade to rice stir cook for 5 Minutes then season to taste with salt & pepper. Then remove from heat and then transfer to a large serving platter garnish with fresh chopped parsley then serve on dinner plates.

CARIBBEAN STYLE CRAB AND CRAWFISH OVER RICE

Makes 5 servings

Ingredients:

2	1 pound pkg crawfish tail meat
2	1 pound can jumbo lump crab meat
½	cup lime juice
¼	cup vegetable oil
1	large red onion, chopped
2	tablespoons garlic, chopped
2	Scotch bonnets chili peppers, seeded and chopped
2	green bell peppers, seeded and chopped
3	teaspoons curry powder
2 ½	cups jasmine rice, cooked
3	cups coconut milk
1	cup Bacardi gold rum
1	cup Champagne
1	cup Hennessey cognac
	New groove seasoning or salt & pepper, to taste

Procedure:

In a large bowl add crawfish, crabmeat, and lime juice champagne, rum, cognac set aside in a large 10 qt Dutch oven

Over medium heat add oil, red onion, garlic, scotch bonnets chili peppers, green bell peppers stir in curry powder cook 3 minutes

Then add rice, marinade, coconut milk stir cover and cook over low heat for 20 minutes stir occasionally then add crawfish,

Crabmeat stir cook for 5 minutes season to taste with new groove seasoning blend or salt & pepper then remove from heat

Then transfer crawfish crab mixture to a large serving platter then serve on dinner plates.

Over rice.

THE SEAFOOD "FUSION" HOOKUP

Makes 3 servings

Ingredients:

6	fresh soft shell crabs, cleaned
1 ½	cups all-purpose flour season with new groove seasoning, dredging crabs
1	cup fresh coconut, grated
2	fresh mangos peeled, medium diced
2	fresh medium peaches peeled, medium diced
3	small Thai Chilie peppers seeded, finely chopped
3	tablespoons fresh garlic cloves, chopped
3	tablespoons fresh ginger root peeled, chopped
3	small fresh shallots peeled, finely chopped
⅓	cup pine nuts
1	bunch fresh chervil, chopped
1	bunch fresh Thai basil, chopped
1	12 oz bag field greens, cleaned
⅓	cup olive oil
⅓	cup Cruzan mango rum
⅓	cup knobs creek bourbon
⅓	cup Hennessey cognac
	New groove house seasoning blend, to taste

Procedure:

In a large 12 inch sauté pan over medium high heat add olive oil then add grated coconut, garlic, ginger, shallots, Thai Chilie peppers, pine nuts, Thai basil, chervil

Then sauté for 3 minutes then add soft shell crabs that was dredged in seasoned flour then sauté for 4 minutes per side then add diced mangoes, diced peaches cognac, bourbon, mango rum then with a long stem match ignite the alcohol and then shake pan until flames dies out then season to taste with new groove

House seasoning blend. Then remove from heat to serve soft shell crabs place some field greens on dinner plates then place soft shell crabs on top then

Pour fruit mixture over soft shell crabs and field greens then serve.

FETTUCCINE WITH SHRIMP, GROUPER, ORANGE ROUGHY AND TOMATOES

Makes 6 servings

Ingredients:

¼	cup olive oil
¼	cup fresh onions, finely chopped
¼	cup fresh carrots, finely chopped
¼	cup fresh celery, finely chopped
3	tablespoons garlic cloves, chopped
2	tablespoons fresh ginger, chopped
2	tablespoons fresh lemon grass, finely chopped
⅓	cup all-purpose flour, add to vegetables
9	fresh plum tomatoes, chopped
2	cups shrimp stock, see recipe
½	cup Champagne
½	cup French apple brandy (calvados)
½	cup Bacardi Tangerine rum
½	cup Hennessey cognac
1	bunch fresh chervil, chopped
1	bunch fresh tarragon, chopped
1	bunch fresh thyme
1	bunch fresh cinnamon basil, chopped
1	tablespoon red pepper flakes
1	package frozen artichokes hearts, thawed and sliced
1	pound fettuccine pasta, cooked and drained
1	pound jumbo 16/20 shrimp save shells for stock, peeled, devained

1	pound grouper fillet, sliced
1	pound orange roughy fillet, sliced
½	cup fresh lemon basil sliced, for garnish
1	cup Parmesan cheese use vegetable peeler, shavings for garnish
	Salt and pepper, to taste
4	cups water, for stock

Procedure:

First in a 3 qt sauce pan over high heat add water then shrimp shells bring to a boil then reduce heat simmer for 15 minutes then strain shrimp stock

Then put aside then in a large 8 qt Dutch oven over medium high heat add olive oil, onions, carrots, celery stir cook for 3 minutes then add chopped garlic, chopped ginger

Lemon grass then cook for 2 minutes then sprinkle flour over vegetables stir cook for 2 minutes then add plum tomatoes, shrimp stock, champagne, tangerine rum, cognac calvados, chopped chervil, chopped tarragon, chopped cinnamon basil, red pepper flakes, thyme stir bring to a boil then reduce heat to medium cook for 15 minutes stirring frequently then add sliced artichoke hearts, jumbo shrimp, sliced grouper filet, sliced orange roughy filet stir then simmer for 7 minutes then season to taste with salt and pepper

Then pour mixture over cooked fettuccine pasta toss then garnish with sliced lemon basil and parmesan cheese shavings. Then serve.

JUMBO SHRIMP WITH JUMBO LUMP CRAB MEAT COGNAC, RUM AND CHAMPAGNE

Makes 5 servings

Ingredients:

- 2 pounds jumbo 16/20 shrimp save shells for stock, cleaned butter flied
- 2 pounds jumbo lump crab meat
- 1 tablespoon fresh thyme
- 1 tablespoon fresh basil, chopped
- 1 tablespoon fresh oregano, chopped
- 1 tablespoon fresh parsley, chopped
- 3 tablespoons garlic cloves, finely chopped
- 2 tablespoons fresh ginger, finely chopped
- 2 tablespoons fresh lemon grass, finely chopped
- 1 tablespoon crushed red pepper flakes
- 3 tablespoons shallots, finely chopped
- ⅓ cup Bacardi dark rum
- ⅓ cup champagne
- ⅓ cup Hennessey cognac
- 4 cups water, to cook shrimp shells
- ⅓ cup olive oil
- Salt and pepper, to taste
- 2 cups white rice, cooked
- 1 package pasta, cooked and drained

Procedure:

In a large 3 quart sauce pan over high heat add 4 cups of water then add shrimp shells then bring to a boil then reduce heat to medium heat cook for 10 minutes

Then drain shrimp stock then put aside then in a large 8 quart Dutch oven over medium heat add olive oil, crushed red pepper flakes, lemon grass, ginger, garlic, shallots

Cook for 2 minutes then add your shrimp stock, parsley, basil, oregano, thyme, dark rum, champagne, cognac, jumbo lump crab meat, jumbo shrimp stir cook for 5 minutes

Season to taste with salt and pepper. Then remove from heat to serve place rice or pasta on dinner plates then ladle seafood on top then serve.

EAST-WEST STYLE SEAFOOD CREOLE

Makes 6 servings

Ingredients:

½	cup olive oil
2	medium red onions, chopped
¼	cup garlic cloves, chopped
2	medium green peppers, seeded and chopped
2	Red Thai Chilie peppers, seeded and chopped
2	green jalapeno chili peppers, seeded and chopped
2	Red Serrano chili peppers, seeded and chopped
6	celery stalks, chopped
6	medium tomato, whole, diced
4	tablespoons dark brown sugar
2	bay leaves
2	tablespoons fresh thyme
2	tablespoons fresh tarragon, chopped
2	tablespoons fresh parsley, chopped
2	tablespoons fresh ginger, chopped
2	pounds 16/20 jumbo shrimp, shelled and cleaned
2	1 pound cans lobster meat
2	1 pound pkg crawfish tail meat
2	pounds jumbo lump crab meat
1 ½	cups Hennessey cognac
1 ½	cups Bacardi gold rum
1 ½	cups Absolut peppar vodka
1 ½	cups Cabernet Sauvignon
	New groove house seasoning or salt & pepper, to taste
2	cups white rice, cooked

Procedure:

In large 10 qt soup pot over medium-low heat add olive oil, onions, garlic, green peppers, Thai Chile peppers, jalapeno chili peppers

Red Serrano chili peppers ginger. Cook for 5 minutes then add tomatoes, celery, brown sugar, thyme, parsley, tarragon, bay leaves, and cognac

Cabernet sauvignon, gold rum, peppar vodka. Cover and simmer for 13 minutes then add lobster meat, crawfish, crab meat, shrimp cover and simmer

For another 6 minutes season to taste with new groove house seasoning blend or salt & pepper then remove from heat to serve Creole over white rice

CORNMEAL CRUSTED TROUT WITH CITRUS PECAN HAZELNUT BUTTER

Makes 5 servings

Ingredients:

- 3 cups cornmeal, dredging fish
- 2 cups all-purpose flour, dredging fish
- ¼ cup lemon juice, see recipe
- ¼ cup lime juice, see recipe
- ¹⁄₄₅ cup orange juice, see recipe
- 2 tablespoons lemon zest, see recipe
- 2 tablespoons orange zest, see recipe
- 2 tablespoons lime zest, see recipe
- ⅔ cup vegetable oil, for cooking fish
- 1 ½ cups milk
- 5 jumbo eggs
- 5 fresh trout, cleaned and seasoned
- 1 cup hazelnuts, chopped and toasted
- 1 cup pecans, chopped and toasted
- 1 pound sweet cream butter, softened
- New groove seasoning or salt & pepper, to taste
- ¼ cup flat leaf parsley, chopped
- ⅔ cup Champagne

Procedure:

1 In a large food processor add nuts butter lemon juice orange juice lime juice orange zest lime zest lemon zest

Process until smooth put aside procedure 2 in a large bowl add flour seasoned with new groove seasoning blend or salt & pepper

In another large bowl add eggs and milk beat until blended and in another large bowl add cornmeal season with new groove seasoning blend

Or salt & pepper. First dredge trout in flour then in egg milk mixture then cornmeal toss to coat put aside then in large frying pan

Over medium high heat add oil then trout cook for 4 minutes per side then cook the remaining trout transfer trout to a platter

Keep warm then wipe out pan then over medium heat add butter parsley champagne cook for 4 minutes remove from heat pour over trout then serve.

NEW GROOVE SEAFOOD CIOPPINO

Makes 6 servings

Ingredients:

- 3 pounds monkfish, cut 1" thick
- 3 pounds sea bass, cut 1" thick
- 3 pounds 21/25 shrimp, shelled and cleaned
- 3 pounds baby squid, sliced
- 3 pounds bay scallops
- 1 each yellow green red orange bell peppers, rough chopped
- 2 each fennel bulbs, chopped
- 2 cups plum tomatoes
- ¼ cup sun-dried tomatoes, julienne
- 2 tablespoons fennel seed, toasted
- 1 tablespoon crushed red pepper
- 1 cup pine nuts, toasted
- 1 8 ounce bottled clam juice
- 5 tablespoons garlic cloves, chopped
- 5 shallots, sliced
- ⅓ cup olive oil
- 2 cups Jose Cuervo Tequila
- 6 cups water
- 2 cups Leroux Ginger Brandy
- 2 cups Bacardi Gold Rum
- 2 cups champagne
- "New groove house seasoning" or salt and pepper, to taste

Procedure:

In a large 12 qt soup pot over medium high heat add olive oil, garlic, fennel, fennel seed, shallots, bell peppers and pine nuts. Cook for 10 minutes. Next add crushed red pepper, sun-dried tomatoes, clam juice, water, plum tomatoes, champagne, rum, ginger brandy and tequila. Reduce heat to medium low and simmer for 10 minutes. Add monkfish, sea bass, squid, bay scallops and shrimp. Continue to simmer for another 10 minutes. Season to taste with "new groove house seasoning or with salt and pepper. Serve cioppino in bowls with bread and green salad.

Chutneys and Salsas

LOBSTER, SHRIMP AND SCALLOP CURRY WITH TROPICAL SALSA

Makes 4 servings

Ingredients:

- ¼ cup olive oil
- 2 lbs frozen lobster tails, thawed, shelled and sliced
- ½ lb large shrimp, peeled, devained
- ½ lb sea scallops
- 1 tsp fresh ginger, peeled and chopped
- 1 tbsp shallots, chopped
- 1 tbsp garlic, chopped
- 1 tsp lemon peel, chopped
- 1 tsp lime peel, chopped
- 1 tsp ground coriander
- 1 tsp curry powder
- 1 tsp turmeric
- ½ tsp crushed red pepper
- 1 cup clam juice
- 1 cup unsweetened coconut milk
- Salt and pepper, to taste

Procedure:

In a large 8 quart dutch oven over medium heat, add olive oil, lobster, shrimp, scallops, and sauté for 2 minutes. Then add ginger, shallots, garlic, lemon peel, lime peel, coriander, curry powder, turmeric, crushed red pepper. Sauté for 2 minutes, then add clam juice, coconut milk. Cook for 4 minutes. Remove from heat. In a sauté pan, add seafood mixture. Heat, add pasta and toss. Serve with salsa on top or serve with steamed rice with salsa on top. Garnish with chopped parsley.

TROPICAL SALSA

Makes about 2 cups

Ingredients:
- 1 mango, peeled, pitted, diced
- 1 cup diced, peeled cucumber, small
- ¼ cup tomatoes, small diced
- ¼ cup green onions, sliced
- 1 jalapeno chili peppers, finely chopped
- 1 tbsp fresh cilantro, finely chopped
- 1 tbsp fresh mint, finely chopped
- ¼ cup lime juice
- Salt and pepper, to taste

Procedure:

Combine all ingredients in large bowl. Season with salt and pepper, and then chill in Refrigerator until ready to serve

MOROCCAN-CARIBBEAN DUO FUSION SALSA

Makes about 9 cups

Ingredients:

- 2 cups dates, sun dried and chopped, Sun maid brand
- 2 cups prunes, sun dried and chopped, Sun maid brand
- 1 ½ cups fresh shredded coconut
- ¼ cup fresh ginger, minced
- 3 green plantains, diced ¼ inch
- 2 cups cherries, sun dried/chopped, Sun maid brand
- 1 ½ cups mango, diced ¼ inch
- 1 ½ tbsp fresh lemon zest
- 1 ½ tbsp fresh orange zest
- 1 cup toasted crushed almonds
- 1 cup toasted crushed macadamia nuts
- ¼ cup Cruzan coconut rum
- ¼ cup Jacquin's ginger brandy
- 1 ½ tsps cinnamon
- 1 ½ tsps nutmeg
- 1 tsp allspice
- Salt and pepper, to taste

Procedure:

Combine all ingredients into large bowl toss well refrigerate up to 4 hours. Goes great with vanilla or ginger peach ice cream, or fish/seafood.

GRILLED MANGO FUSION CHUTNEY

Makes 5 servings

Ingredients:

3	ripe mangos, skinned and sliced ¼", grilled and diced small
1	papayas, sliced ¼", grilled and diced small
1	medium red Bermuda onion, diced small
1	medium Vidalia onion, diced small
2	cups of golden raisins
1	cup of sweet flake coconut, toasted
3	cups of sun dried sweet dates, diced medium
1 ½	cups of macadamia nuts, crushed and roasted
1 ½	cups sliced almonds, toasted
6	Thai chilies, seeded and diced small
3 ½	tbsp lemon grass, chopped finely
2	tbsp each lemon, lime and orange zest
3/12	tbsp fresh ginger, chopped finely
1 ⅓	cups dark brown sugar
1	tbsp nutmeg
1	tbsp cinnamon
1	tbsp all spice
¼	cup Cruzan dark rum
⅔	cup Cruzan coconut rum
¼	cup Cruzan pineapple rum
	Nice splash of Jacquin's ginger brandy
	Salt and pepper, to taste

Procedure:

In large 6 quart dutch oven over medium heat combine all ingredients except mango, and papaya and mix well. Cook 30 minutes. In the last 5 minutes, add mangos. Cook additional 5 minutes, and then transfer to bowl. Serve with baked or grilled fish or chicken. Cook 10 minutes. Serve chilled or warm.

ASIAN FIRE CHUTNEY
LACED WITH GINGER BRANDY AND PEPPAR VODKA

Makes 6 servings

Ingredients:
- 1 medium pineapple, peeled and diced
- 4 medium Asian pears, peeled and diced
- 8 medium Thai chili peppers fire roasted, seeded and diced
- 1 medium white onion, diced small
- 5 medium ears of sweet white corn grilled, cut off cob
- Zest and juice from 4 mandarin oranges, seeds removed
- Zest and juice from 3 limes, seeds removed
- 3 tablespoons fresh ginger, minced
- 3 tablespoons fresh lemon grass, minced
- ¼ cup coconut milk
- 1 cup coconut flakes, lightly toasted
- 1 cup sliced almonds, lightly toasted
- ½ cup peanuts, lightly toasted
- ¼ cups dried dates soaked in Capt. Morgan spiced rum, drained optional
- ⅓ cup dark brown sugar
- ¼ cup Absolut Peppar vodka
- ¼ cup Leroux Ginger Brandy
- 2 teaspoons all spice
- 2 teaspoons yellow curry powder

Procedure:

Combine all ingredients into a large bowl, toss and blend well. Chill up to 4 hours. Serve cold or at room temperature. Goes great with fish, seafood and chicken.

SHOTGUN CARIBBEAN SALSA
LACED WITH GINGER BRANDY AND RUM

Makes 6 servings

Ingredients:

1	medium pineapple, peeled and diced
1	medium mango, peeled and diced
5	medium Serrano peppers, seeded and diced
5	medium jalapeño peppers, seeded and diced
5	medium Poblano peppers, seeded and diced
	Zest and juice from 3 blood oranges, seeds removed
	Zest and juice from 3 limes, seeds removed
3	tablespoons fresh ginger, minced
3	tablespoons fresh lemon grass, minced
1	small bunch of peppermint stems removed, finely chopped
1 ¼	cups coconut milk
1	cup coconut flakes, lightly toasted
2	medium green plantains, peeled and diced
1 ¼	cups dried cherries soaked in red wine, drained
1 ¼	cups dried dates soaked in spiced rum, drained
⅓	cup dark brown sugar
¼	cup Malibu coconut rum
¼	cup Cruzan Mango Rum
¼	cup Leroux Ginger Brandy
1	teaspoon all spice
1	teaspoon nutmeg
1	teaspoon cinnamon

Procedure:

Combine all ingredients into a large bowl, toss and blend well. Chill up to 4 hours. Serve cold or at room temperature. Goes great with fish, seafood and chicken.

CUCUMBER-BERMUDA ONION GINGER SALSA

Makes 6 servings

Ingredients:

- 2 large cucumbers peeled, diced small
- 1 large Bermuda onion, sliced 1/4" thick
- 4 tablespoons fresh ginger, finely chopped
- 4 tablespoons fresh lemon grass, finely chopped
- 8 medium Serrano pepper, seeded and diced

For Marinade:

- ½ cup olive oil
- ¼ cup champagne wine vinegar
- ¼ cup Leroux Ginger Brandy
- ¼ cup Captain Morgan Spiced Rum
- 3 tablespoons smoked chipotle paste
- Zest from 2 limes
- Zest from 1 blood orange
- 3 tablespoons fresh ginger
- Salt and pepper, to taste

Procedure:

Combine all marinade ingredients into food processor and blend until smooth. Then transfer to bowl and chill for 1 hour. Meanwhile in a large bowl, combine all ingredients for salsa. Toss well and chill for about 1 hour. Then combine marinade to salsa and toss well to blend then garnish with fried Asian noodles.

GRILLED MANGO WITH FUSION CHUTNEY

Makes 8 servings

Ingredients:

3	medium ripe mangos peeled, sliced grilled, diced small
1	medium ripe papaya, peeled, sliced grilled, diced small
1	medium pineapple peeled, sliced grilled, diced small
1 ¼	cups coconut flakes, lightly toasted
¼	cup fresh ginger, minced
2	medium avocado, peeled and diced
2 ½	cups macadamia nuts, toasted and crushed
1	cup almond slices, toasted
2 ½	tablespoons each zest of lemon, lime and orange
1	cup light brown sugar
⅓	cup Myers's dark rum
⅓	cup Cruzan Coconut Rum
1 ¼	cups Cruzan Mango Rum
2 ½	teaspoons yellow curry powder
2	teaspoons cinnamon
2	teaspoons nutmeg

Procedure:

Combine all ingredients into a large pot and cook for 8 to 10 minutes over medium heat stirring often. Finish with 2 tablespoons of sweet cream butter. Transfer to bowl and serve. Serve with fish, seafood or chicken.

NEW GROOVE HOUSE STYLE FUSION SALSA

Makes 8 servings

Ingredients:

1	medium pineapple, peeled and diced
2	medium mango, peeled and diced
1	medium papaya, peeled and diced
1	medium honeydew melon, peeled and diced
1 ¼	cups dried cherries soaked in cherry brandy, drained
1 ¼	cups dried dates soaked in spiced rum, drained
1 ¼	cups blackberries
1 ¼	cups raspberries
10	medium Serrano pepper, seeded and diced
10	medium jalapeño peppers, seeded and diced
2	medium yellow bell pepper, seeded and diced
2	medium red bell pepper, seeded and diced
1	medium Bermuda onion, diced small
1	small Vidalia onion, diced small
⅔	cup fresh ginger, minced
⅓	cup fresh garlic, minced
1	cup light brown sugar
	Season to taste with "new groove house seasoning"
⅔	cup Cruzan Citrus Rum
⅔	cup Captain Morgan Spiced Rum

Procedure:

Combine all ingredients into large bowl and toss and blend well. Chill up to 4 hours before serving. Goes great with fish, seafood and chicken.

Sweets, Desserts and Sweets Desserts

We all know the saying life is uncertain so eat dessert first perhaps There is a lesson to be learned. Dessert is a main event or a decadent. To a great dinner for most people. Desserts is rich smooth creamy and of course sweet in textures and tastes my signature desserts are all homemade. I take great pride in showcasing my desserts because it is the finale.and I want to create for you a memorable finale that will leave a lasting impression. My desserts are artstic creative and innovative in every regard and. I pay special attention to the sweet tooth. I use the finest confections, sugars, creams, chocolate,fruits, spices, liqueurs and flavorings. To create pure fusion style sweet decadence.

FUSZION STYLE MADELEINES
GANT COPYRIGHTED 2003 & 2004

Makes 6 servings.

Ingredients:
- 1 ½ cups sugar, add to eggs
- 3 cups flour, all-purpose, sifted
- 2 teaspoons baking powder, siffed with flour
- 2 sticks sweet cream butter, softened
- 5 jumbo eggs, whisk
- 2 tablespoons orange zest, see recipe
- 2 tablespoons vanilla rum, see recipe
- 2 tablespoons vodka, see recipe
- 2 tablespoons hazelnut liquor, see recipe
- 2 tablespoons cognac, see recipe
- 2 tablespoons orange curacao, see recipe
- 2 tablespoons orange juice, see recipe

Procedure:

IN A LARGE MIXING BOWL WHISK TOGETHER EGGS, AND SUGAR UNTIL THICK AND PALE YELLOW THEN SIFT FLOUR, AND BAKING POWDER OVER MIXTURE THEN FOLD IN FLOUR, BAKING POWDER THEN ADD BUTTER, ORANGE JUICE, ORANGE ZEST, ORANGE CURACAO, COGNAC, VANILLA RUM, HAZELNUT LIQUOR, VODKA MIX WELL THEN COVER AND REFRIGERATE FOR 30 MINUTES THEN PRE HEAT OVEN AT 425°F THEN GENEROUSLY GREASE MADELEINE MOLDS AND DUST WITH FLOUR THEN SPOON MIXTURE INTO MOLDS SO THEY ARE NO MORE THEN TWO THIRDS FULL BAKE AT 425°F FOR 7 MINUTES OR UNTIL PUFFED THEN REDUCE OVEN TEMPERATURE TO 325°F THEN BAKE ANOTHER 7 MINUTES OR UNTIL PALE GOLD ON TOP AND SLIGHTLY DARKER AROUND THE EDGES REMOVE FROM MOLDS TRANSFER TO WIRE RACK LET COOL MAKES ABOUT 40 MADELEINES.

Per serving (excluding unknown items): 530.3 Calories; 8.6g Fat (14.8% calories from fat); 11.8g Protien; 99.6g Carbohydrates; 190mg Cholesterol; 2014mg Sodium. Exchanges: 3 grain (Starch); 1 Lean Meat; 3 ½ Fruit; 1 Fat; 3 ½ other Carbohydrates.

NEW GROOVE FUSZION STYLE POUND CAKE

RICKY GANT COPYRIGHT 2019

Ingredients:

- 3   cups All-Purpose Flour siffed
- 1   Teaspoon salt siffed with Flour
- 3   Teaspoons Baking powder siffed with Flour
- 2 ½ cups sugar add to butter
- 3   sticks sweet cream butter room temperature
- 1 ¼ cups Buttermilk
- 6   Jumbo Eggs room temperature
- 2   Tablespoons Bacardi Black Rum
- 2   Tablespoons Absolut Vodka Vanilla
- 2   Tablespoons Jim Beam Black Bourbon
- 2   Tablespoons Hennessy Black Cognac
- 2   Tablespoons Kahlua Coffee Liqueur

Procedure:

First Pre-heat oven at 325°F Then Grease Flour in a 10 cup Bundt pan then put aside. Then in a Large mixing bowl siff together Flour, salt baking powder Twice then put aside then in another Large mixing bowl mix together Butter, Sugar until blended then add your flour mixture and buttermilk stir well then add your eggs one at a time stir well then add your eggs one at a time stir well after each one then stir in Black Rum, Vanilla Vodka, Black Bourbon, Black Cognac, Coffee Liqueur mix well then pour cake Batter into Bundt Pan Bake at 325°F for 1 hour and 15 minutes or until Toothpick comes out clean. Let cool then remove cake from Bundt Pan. To serve cake slice cake put on plates serve with coffee or Milk.

NEW GROOVE BLACKBERRY AND RASPBERRY SHORT-CAKE

Makes 8 servings

Ingredients:

For fruit

¼	cup Smirnoff raspberry vodka
¼	cup jacquin's blackberry brandy
1	cup granulated sugar
2	packages fresh raspberries
2	packages fresh black raspberries

For cake

2 ½	cups all-purpose flour
1	tsp salt
2	tsp baking powder
3	tbsp Cruzan vanilla rum
3	tbsp Jacquin's blackberry brandy
1 ½	cups sugar
2 ½	sticks sweet butter, softened
1 ¼	cups milk
5	jumbo eggs

For whipped cream

2	tbsp jacquin's blackberry brandy
2	tbsp Cruzan vanilla rum
½	cup powdered sugar
1	pint heavy whipping cream

Procedure:

First in a medium size bowl combine blackberries, raspberries, sugar, raspberry vodka blackberry brandy toss well put in fridge then grease and flour two 8 by 2 round cake pans then put aside then sift together flour, salt, baking powder twice then in a large bowl add sweet butter soften and sugar beat until smooth then stir in flour mixture stir to blend then add milk stir to blend then stir in eggs one at a time then stir in vanilla rum, blackberry brandy stir until well blended then pour cake batter into cake pans bake at 350*F for 35 minutes

Or until toothpick comes out clean let cool then in a large mixing bowl combine powdered sugar, blackberry brandy and vanilla rum heavy whipping cream then whip at high speed for about 5 minutes or until stiff to put together cake place 1 cake layer on a large plate then spoon fruit on then ladle some of juice from the fruit over the cake then top with whipped cream then place the second layer on top spoon on fruit ladle some of the juice on top then top with the remaining whipped cream then garnish with berries. Then put short cake in the refrigerator.

Until ready to serve to serve slice short-cake put on desert plates serve with cold milk, coffee

FUSZION STYLE TIRAMISU
GANT COPYRIGHTED 2003 & 2004

Makes 10 servings.

Ingredients:

For custard

4	cups milk, mix together
2 ½	cups sugar, mix together
15	Jumbo egg yolks, see recipe
½	cup cornstarch, see recipe
½	cup sugar, see recipe
⅓	cup sweet maderia wine, add to eggs
⅓	cup coffee liqueur, add to eggs
⅓	cup spice tum, add to eggs
⅓	cup cognac, add to eggs
1	pint heavy whipping cream, mix together
⅓	cup powdered sugar, mix together
2	pounds marscapone cheese, to top custard
2	cups expresso coffee, to dip madeleins
1 ¼	cups cocoa powder, to dust top
1	tablespoon ground nutmeg, to dust top
1	tablespoon ground cinnamon, to dust top

madeleine recipe to follow and in the procedure it should say then take your madeleines dip them in expresso coffee

Procedure:

IN A LARGE 4 QT SAUCE PAN OVER LOW HEAT ADD MILK AND 2 ½ CUPS SUGAR STIR COOK UNTIL WARM

DO NOT BOIL THEN IN A LARGE MIXING BOWL COMBINE EGG YOLKS, ½ SUGAR, CORNSTARCH

BEAT WITH A WIRE WISK UNTIL SMOOTH THEN ADD THE WARM MILK TO THE EGG MIXTURE THEN ADD MIXTURE BACK TO SAUCEPAN THEN ADD COFFEE LIQUOR, MADERIA WINE, SPICE RUM, COGNAC STIR

COOK OVER LOW HEAT UNTIL THICKEN ALWAYS STIRRING THEN REMOVE FROM HEAT PLACE N A BOWL THEN CHILL FOR ABOUT 2 HOURS THEN WITH A ELECTRIC STAND MIXER FITTED WITH A WIRE WISK

IN A LARGE MIXING BOWL BEAT HEAVY WHIPPING CREAM WITH POWDERED SUGAR BEAT UNTIL STIFF THEN CHILL WHIPPED CREAM ONCE CHILLED FOLD WHIPPED CREAM INTO CUSTARD UNTIL WELL BLENDED

THEN TAKE YOUR MEDELEINES DIP THEM IN EXPRESSO COFFEE THEN PLACE THEM IN A 9 BY 13 BAKING DISH THEN COVER WITH CUSTARD THEN MARSCAPONE CHEESE THEN MORE MADELEINES THEN CUSTARD AND MARSCAPONE CHEESE UNTIL YOU FILL BAKING DISH THE DUST THE TOP OF THE TIRAMISU WITH COCOA POWDER, CINNAMON, NUTMEG THEN CHILL TIRAMISU UNTIL READY TO SERVE CUT INTO SQUARES

Per serving (excluding unkown items): 663.5 Calories; 30.3g Fat(41.1% calories fron fat); 10.6g Protien; 87.1g Carbohydrate; 398mg Cholesterol; 81mg Sodium. Exchanges: 1 Grain(Starch); ½ Lean Meat; ½ Non-Fat Milk; 4 Fruit; 5 ½ Fat; 4 ½ Other C

NEW GROOVE PEACH MANGO SHORTCAKE
WITH A ORANGE CUSTARD SAUCE

Makes 8 servings

Ingredients:
- 2 ½ cups all-purpose flour
- ½ tsp salt, add to flour
- 2 ¼ tsp baking powder, add to flour
- ½ tsp ground cinnamon, add to flour
- ½ tsp ground nutmeg, add to flour
- 2 cups granulated sugar
- 1 cup milk
- 1 tbsp Cruzan vanilla rum
- 1 tbsp Bacardi dark rum
- 1 tbsp Barton peach schnapps
- 1 tbsp amaretto liqueur
- 5 jumbo eggs, room temp
- 2 ¼ sticks sweet butter, softened
- 3 medium fresh peaches, sliced
- 2 medium fresh mangos, peeled and sliced
- ½ cup granulated sugar
- ¼ cup Bacardi dark rum
- ¼ cup Barton peach schnapps
- ¼ cup amaretto liqueur

For orange custard
- 2 cups milk
- 1 cup granulated sugar
- 6 jumbo egg yolks
- ⅓ cup cornstarch
- 1 cup granulated sugar
- 3 tbsp orange zest

½	cup orange juice
¼	cup Orange Curacao liqueur
2	tbsp sweet butter

For whipped cream
1	pint heavy whipping cream
½	cup powdered sugar
2	tbsp amaretto liqueur

Procedure:

First slice peaches and mangos then put fruit in medium size bowl then add sugar rum, peach schnapps, amaretto stir then put in fridge then preheat oven at 350°F then grease and flour two 9 inch by 1 ½ inch round cake pans put aside then in a large bowl combine sugar, butter mix until smooth then in a medium bowl combine flour, cinnamon, nutmeg, salt baking powder stir then add flour mixture to the sugar and butter mixture stir then add milk mix well then stir in eggs one at a time mix until smooth then stir in amaretto, peach schnapps, vanilla rum stir well until well blended then pour cake batter into pans bake at 350*F for 30 to 35 minutes or until toothpick comes out clean then remove cake from oven let cool then in a 4 qt sauce pan over medium heat add milk sugar stir cook until heated through do not boil then in a large Bowl combine egg yolks cornstarch sugar orange juice, Orange Curacao mix until smooth then slowly pour the heated milk into the orange mixture stir then add mixture back to the saucepan cook over low heat until thick remove from heat stir in two tablespoons sweet then with a hand blender blend until smooth then chill. In a large mixing bowl combine powdered sugar amaretto heavy whipping cream whip at high speed for 5 minutes or until stiff to put together shortcake place one Cake layer on a large plate then spoon on fruit then spoon on custard then top with whipped cream then place the other cake layer on top spoon on fruit then custard Then whipped cream then garnish with some of the sliced fruit. Then put short-cake in the refrigerator until ready to serve to serve cut short-cake place on desert plates Then serve with cold milk or coffee.

NEW GROOVE CHOCOLATE COLD SWEAT SHORTCAKE

Makes 9 servings

Ingredients:
For chocolate shortcake recipe

3 ½	cups all-purpose flour
½	tsp salt, add to flour
2 ½	tsp baking powder, add to flour
2 ½	cups granulated sugar
3	sticks sweet butter, room temp
5	1 oz baking chocolate squares, melted
6	jumbo eggs, room temp
¼	cup Cruzan vanilla rum
½	cup milk
¼	cup frangelico liqueur
4	small Serrano peppers seeded, finely chopped
4	small Habanero Chile seeded, finely chopped
1	cup hazelnuts, finely ground

For fruit

1	pint blueberries
1	pint raspberries
1	pint boysenberries
1	pint blackberries
½	cup granulated sugar
⅓	cup Cruzan vanilla rum

For mint custard recipe

1 ½	cups milk
1 ½	cups heavy cream

2	cups granulated sugar
2	tbsp sweet butter
7	jumbo egg yolks
½	cup cornstarch
1	bunch fresh mint leaves save some for garnish, chopped fine
2	tbsp cream de mint liqueur

For whipped cream

1	pint heavy whipping cream
½	cup powdered sugar
2	tbsp Smirnoff raspberry vodka

Procedure:

First preheat oven at 375°F then in a large bowl combine blueberries, raspberries, boysenberries, blackberries, sugar, vanilla rum mix well then chill then grease and flour 3 9 inch by 1 ½ inch round cake pans put aside then in a large bowl sift together flour, salt, baking powder. Then with a large mixer fitted with a paddle in a mixing bowl

Combine sugar, butter, melted chocolate beat at medium speed until fluffy then add flour, ground hazelnuts, Serrano Chile peppers, habanero Chile peppers at low speed mix until blended then add milk stir at low speed then add your eggs one at a time until blended stir in frangelico liqueur, vanilla rum mix until blended at low speed then

Pour cake batter into pans bake at 375°F for 30 to 35 minutes or until toothpick comes out clean. Then remove cake from oven let cool then in a 4 qt sauce pan over low heat

Add your milk, heavy cream and 1 cup of sugar stir cook over low heat until warm do not boil then in a large bowl combine egg yolks, one cup sugar, cornstarch with a wire whisk

Beat until smooth then temper the egg mixture by whisking in some of the warm milk and cream then return mixture to heat cook until thicken always stirring bout 10 minutes then

Then remove from heat stir in butter, cream de mint liqueur fresh mint then with a hand blender blend until smooth then pour custard into a bowl chill then with a large mixer fitted

With a wire whisk in a large mixing bowl add powdered sugar, raspberry vodka, and heavy whipping cream whip at high speed for about 5 minutes until stiff to put together shortcake

Place one cake layer on a large plate then spoon on mint custard then fruit then whipped cream then place the other cake layer on top spoon on mint custard then fruit then whipped cream

Then put the last cake layer on top spoon on custard then fruit then whipped cream then garnish with some fresh mint leaves. Then put short-cake in the refrigerator until ready to serve.

To serve slice short-cake place on desert plates then serve with ice cold milk or coffee.

NEW GROOVE BREAD PUDDING
WITH DATES NUTS AND CRANBERRIES

Makes 10 servings

Ingredients:
- 1 pound loaf potato bread, torn into pieces
- 1 cup dates, chopped
- 1 cup dried cranberries
- ½ cup pecans, chopped
- ½ cup hazelnuts, chopped
- 3 cups milk
- ½ tsp ground nutmeg
- ½ tsp ground cinnamon
- ¼ cup Burnett vanilla vodka
- 1 ½ cups granulated sugar
- ¼ cup Orange Curacao liqueur

For orange custard sauce
- 2 cups milk
- ½ cup heavy cream
- 1 cup granulated sugar
- 8 jumbo egg yolks
- ⅓ cup cornstarch
- ¾ cup granulated sugar
- 1 ½ cups orange juice
- 2 tsp orange zest
- ¼ cup Orange Curacao liqueur

Procedure:

First put torn bread in a large bowl then in another bowl add milk, sugar, nutmeg, cinnamon, vanilla vodka, Orange Curacao mix well the pour over bread

Then stir in nuts, dates, cranberries let stand for 10 minutes then pour bread mixture into a greased 9 by 13 inch baking pan. Bake at 350°F for about 2

Hours or until knife comes out clean. For orange custard sauce first in a 3 qt over low heat add milk, cream, sugar stir heat up milk & cream until warm then in a large bowl add sugar, cornstarch, egg yolks, orange juice mix well then add warm milk & cream slowly to the egg mixture then return to heat

Cook over low heat stirring until thick then remove form heat add ½ stick butter, Orange Curacao liqueur then with a hand blender blend until smooth

Then stir in orange zest then chill serve sauce with bread pudding. To serve cut bread pudding into squares then place on desert plates then spoon

For orange custard sauce first in a 3 quart sauce pan over low heat add milk, cream, sugar.

NEW GROOVE CHERRY COBBLER
WITH RUM CHERRY BRANDY AND CHAMPAGNE

Makes 10 servings

Ingredients:

4	pounds fresh cherries or frozen, pitted
2	cups granulated sugar
½	tsp ground mace
1	tsp ground cinnamon
3	tbsp cornstarch
1	cup Kirshwasser cherry brandy
½	cup Bacardi dark rum
½	cup Champagne

For biscuit topping

5	cups all-purpose flour
1	tsp salt, mix with flour
2	tsp baking soda, mix with flour
2	tsp baking powder, mix with flour
2	tbsp granulated sugar, mix with flour
2	sticks sweet butter, cut in 1" cubes
2 ¼	cups buttermilk

Procedure:

Preheat oven at 450°F in a large bowl combine cherries, cornstarch, mace, cinnamon, sugar, cherry brandy, dark rum, champagne then mix well then pour the fruit into a large three quart baking dish

Then put aside. For biscuit topping in large bowl combine five cups flour one teaspoon of salt two teaspoons baking soda two teaspoons baking powder two tablespoons sugar stir then cut in two sticks of sweet butter cut into pieces with a pastry cutter then work the dough until flour looks the size of small peas then pour in two quarter and cups of buttermilk mix well until soft dough forms then place dough on a floured board then knead dough for three minutes then roll out dough to a half inch thick then cut dough with a biscuit cutter or a small glass

Then place biscuits on top of fruit then top with a little sugar. Then bake cobbler at 450°F for fifty five minutes then remove cherry cobbler from the oven let cool serve warm.

To serve spoon cherry cobbler into a bowl then top with 3 scoops vanilla ice cream then serve with coffee.

NEW GROOVE GINGER CHAMPAGNE LEMON CAKE

Makes 8 servings

Ingredients:
- 2 ½ cups all-purpose flour
- ½ tsp salt, add to flour
- 2 tsp baking powder, add to flour
- ¼ cup fresh lemon zest
- 1 tbsp lemon extract
- 1 ½ cups granulated sugar
- 1 cup unsweetened coconut flakes
- 5 jumbo eggs, room temp
- 4 sticks sweet butter, softened
- ¼ cup jacquin's ginger brandy
- ¼ cup Champagne
- ¼ cup coconut milk
- 2 tsp ground nutmeg

Recipe for frosting / glaze
- 1 pint heavy whipping cream
- ¼ cup powdered sugar
- 1 tsp cream of tartar
- 1 tsp candied ginger, minced
- 1 tbsp Cruzan vanilla rum
- 1 tbsp Jacquin's ginger brandy
- 1 tsp lemon extract
- 1 tbsp lemon zest
- 1 tbsp orange zest
- 1 tbsp lime zest

Procedure:

Preheat oven at 350°F then grease and flour two 9 inch by 1 ½ inch round cake pans then put aside then in a large bowl combine butter, sugar beat until smooth then add flour, baking powder salt, candied ginger, nutmeg, coconut flakes, eggs, lemon zest, lemon extract, ginger brandy, champagne, coconut milk mix well until well blended then pour cake batter into pans. Bake at 350°F.

for 35 to 40 minutes or until toothpick comes out clean then remove cake from oven let cool then remove cake from pan put aside then in a large mixing bowl add powdered sugar, cream of tartar, candied ginger, ginger brandy, vanilla rum, lemon zest, lime zest, orange zest, heavy whipping cream beat at high speed until stiff about 6 minutes then frost the cake then put cake in the refrigerator until ready

To serve cake. To serve slice cake place on desert plates serve.

With cold milk or coffee.

NEW GROOVE TRIPLE CHOCOLATE CHIP BAR COOKIES

Makes 8 servings

Ingredients:
- 3 cups all-purpose flour
- 2 sticks sweet butter, softened
- 2 cups light brown sugar
- 1 cup sugar
- 1 ½ tsp baking soda, mix with flour
- 1 ½ tsp ground cinnamon, mix with flour
- 2 tsp baking powder, mix with flour
- ½ tsp salt, mix with flour
- 3 jumbo eggs
- ½ cup hazelnuts, chopped
- ½ cup pecans, chopped
- 1 cup coconut flakes, shredded
- 1 cup dried cranberries
- 1 12 oz package peanut butter chips
- 1 12 oz package double chocolate chips
- 1 12 oz package white chocolate chips
- 3 tbsp Bacardi dark rum
- 3 tbsp Hennessey cognac

Procedure:

Preheat oven at 350°F in a large bowl combine butter, sugar, brown sugar mix until smooth then add eggs stir until blended then in a medium size bowl add flour, salt, baking soda, baking powder, cinnamon stir then add the flour mixture to the large bowl with eggs, sugars, butter blend well then add cognac, rum, nuts,

Coconut flakes, cranberries, peanut butter chips, double chocolate chips, white chocolate chips mix well then spray a 9 x 13 baking dish with cooking spray then add cookie dough bake at 350°F for 35 minutes then remove from oven let cool then cut into sq. then place in a airtight container

To serve place cookies on desert plates then serve with coffee, cold milk or ice cream.

NEW GROOVE AMARETTO CHEESE COOKIES

Makes 3 ½ dozen cookies

Ingredients:

2 ¾	cups all-purpose flour
½	cup light brown sugar
1	cup butter
2	sticks sweet butter, softened
1	8 oz package cream cheese, softened
3	jumbo eggs
1	tsp vanilla extract
1	cup almonds, sliced
¼	cup amaretto liquor
1	tsp salt, mix with flour
2	tsp baking soda, mix with flour
2	tsp baking powder, mix with flour

Procedure:

Preheat oven at 375°F in a medium size bowl combine flour, salt, baking soda, baking powder, stir then put aside then in a large bowl combine both sugars, cream cheese, butter

Eggs, vanilla extract, amaretto liquor, mix until smooth then stir in sliced almonds, and flour mixture mix well place one level tablespoon of cookie dough on noon-stick sheet.

Bake at 375°F for 10 minutes then remove cookies from oven let cool then put cookies in a airtight container makes about 3 ½ dozen. To serve place cookies on desert plates

Serve with vanilla ice cream, cold milk or coffee.

NEW GROOVE FRUIT COBBLER WITH PEACH SCHNAPPS AND RUM

Makes 10 servings

Ingredients:

1	pound	fresh peach, whole, med., pitted and sliced
1	pound	fresh nectarines, pitted and sliced
1	pound	fresh plums red or black, pitted and sliced
1	pint	fresh black raspberries
2	cups	granulated sugar
2	tsp	ground cinnamon
1	tsp	ground nutmeg
1 ½	cups	Barton peach schnapps
½	cup	Bacardi gold rum

For pie crust

2 ½	cups	all-purpose flour
1	cup	shortening, add to flour
5	tbsp	cold water
½	tsp	salt, add to flour

Procedure:

First preheat oven at 375°F then in a large bowl combine peaches, nectarines, plum, black raspberries, sugar, cinnamon, nutmeg, gold rum, peach schnapps, then mix well then place fruit mixture

In a 9 by 13 baking dish then put aside then in a large bowl combine salt, flour, stir then add shortening then with pastry blender mix dough until dough looks like the size of small peas then add water

Stir with a fork then roll out dough place pie dough over the top of the baking dish then seal cut small slits in pie crust to let out steam. Then sprinkle sugar on top bake at 375°F for 1 hour and 15 minutes then remove fruit cobbler from oven let cool serve warm to serve spoon fruit cobbler into a bowl then top with 2 scoops of vanilla ice cream then serve with cold milk or coffee.

NEW GROOVE FRENCH APPLE PIE WITH APPLEJACK BRANDY

Makes 8 servings

Ingredients:
- 3 pounds Granny Smith apples, peeled and sliced
- 1 tsp ground ginger
- 1 tsp ground nutmeg
- 2 tsp ground cinnamon
- 2 cups granulated sugar
- 1 cup raisins
- 1 cup hazelnuts
- ¼ cup champagne
- 2 tbsp cornstarch
- 1 cup laird's applejack brandy
- ¼ cup Bacardi gold rum
- ⅓ cup Hennessy cognac
- 1 stick sweet butter cut into pieces

For pie crust
- 1 cup shortening
- 5 tbsp cold water
- ½ tsp salt
- 1 jumbo egg, add to milk
- ¼ cup milk
- 3 cups all-purpose flour

Procedure:

First preheat oven at 425°F then in a large bowl add sliced apples, ginger, nutmeg, cinnamon, hazelnuts, cornstarch applejack brandy gold rum, raisins, champagne and cognac

Sugar then mix well then put aside in another large bowl combine flour, salt, stir then add shortening then with a pastry blender work the dough until dough looks like the size of small peas then add water then stir with a fork then divide dough roll out dough place in a 9 ½ inch pie plate add pie filling top with butter then place pie crust on top seal then make small cuts on top of pie crust let out steam then in a small bowl combine egg milk stir then brush the top of pie with the egg milk mixture bake at 425°F for 55 minutes then remove pie from oven let cool to serve cut pie into wedges place pie

On plates then top with a scoop vanilla ice cream then serve with cold milk or coffee.

NEW GROOVE CHOCOLATE APPLE ZUCCHINI CAKE

Makes 10 servings

Ingredients:

2	sticks sweet butter, softened
1	cup safflower oil
1	cup sugar
1 ½	cups light brown sugar
4	jumbo eggs, room temp
1	tbsp vanilla extract
1	cup buttermilk
1	tsp ground cinnamon, sifted with flour
½	tsp salt, sifted with flour
2 ½	tsp baking powder, sifted with flour
2	tsp baking soda, sifted with flour
3 ⅔	cups all-purpose flour, sifted
½	cup cocoa powder, sifted with flour
1	cup walnuts, chopped
2 ¼	cups grated apples, grated
2 ¼	cups grated zucchini, grated
2	tbsp Smirnoff vodka
2	tbsp Bacardi gold rum
2	tbsp French apple brandy (calvados)

Chocolate frosting recipe for cake

1	stick sweet butter, melted
4	1 oz baking chocolate squares, melted
1	box powdered sugar, see recipe
5	tbsp milk, see recipe
1	tbsp Smirnoff vodka see recipe
1	tbsp Bacardi gold rum see recipe
1	tbsp French apple brandy (calvados) see recipe

Procedure:

Preheat oven to 350°F then grease and flour dust a 9 by 13 baking pan then in a large bowl add butter oil, sugar, brown sugar mix until smooth then beat in eggs, vanilla, vodka, rum, French apple brandy mix until smooth then sift together the dry ingredients flour, baking soda, baking powder, cinnamon, salt, cocoa powder then add to the creamed mixture stir to blend then add zucchini, apples, chopped walnuts

Mix until well blended then pour cake batter into pan bake for 1 hour and 15 minutes or until toothpick comes out clean let cake cool in pan recipe for chocolate frosting in a large mixing bowl add one stick sweet butter melted then add four one oz chocolate squares milted mix until smooth then sift one box of powdered sugar into mixing bowl then add five tablespoons of milk and one tablespoon of each vodka, rum, French apple brandy then with a hand blender mix until smooth then frost cake, then refrigerate cake until ready to serve to serve cake cut into squares then place on desert plates then serve with coffee, cold milk, or vanilla ice cream.

NEW GROOVE ANISETTE TOAST

Makes 3 1/2 dozen toast

Ingredients:
- 7 jumbo eggs
- 3 ½ cups all-purpose flour
- 1 ½ cups granulated sugar
- ¼ cup anise liquor
- ¼ cup Bol's Orange Curacao
- ¼ cup Bacardi gold rum
- 1 cup crushed almonds, toasted
- 1 cup crushed hazelnuts, toasted
- 1 ¼ cups Canola oil
- 1 tbsp baking powder

Procedure:

Preheat oven at 350°F for 15 minutes grease and flour dust two sheet pans then put aside then in a large bowl add sugar, canola oil mix well to blend then add flour baking powder, anise liquor, gold rum, orange Curacao, almonds, hazelnuts mix well to blend then transfer to baking sheets bake at 350°F for 30 minutes then remove from oven when toast are golden brown then cut / slice toast

Return toasts to baking sheets then lightly brown on both sides about 4 minutes per side makes about 3 ½ dozen. Then remove anisette toast from oven let cool then put anisette toast in a

Airtight container to serve place anisette toast on desert plates serves with coffee.

NEW GROOVE BANANA FOSTERS COOKIES

Makes 5 dozen cookies

Ingredients:
- 4 ¾ cups all-purpose flour
- 1 tsp salt
- 2 tsp baking soda
- 1 tsp ground cinnamon
- 1 tsp ground nutmeg
- 2 ¾ cups light brown sugar
- 3 jumbo eggs
- 2 sticks sweet butter, softened
- 3 medium ripe bananas, mashed
- 1 cup hazelnuts, chopped
- 1 cup pecans, chopped
- 1 cup shredded coconut flakes
- 1 12 oz package peanut butter chips
- 1 12 oz package chocolate chips
- 4 tsp fresh mint, finely chopped
- 2 tsp Cruzan vanilla rum
- ⅓ cup jacquin's banana liqueur
- 2 tbsp Bacardi gold rum
- 2 tbsp Bacardi coconut rum
- 2 tbsp Hennessey cognac

Procedure:

First preheat oven at 350°F then in a large mixed fitted with a paddle in the mixing bowl combine sugar, butter, bananas then beat at medium speed until light and fluffy

Then add flour, salt, baking soda, cinnamon, nutmeg, eggs then mix at low speed until well blended then add hazelnuts, pecans, coconut flakes, peanut butter chips

Chocolate chips, fresh mint, vanilla rum, banana liqueur, gold rum, coconut rum, cognac. The mix at low speed until well blended then drop one level tablespoon on ungreased baking sheet bake at 350*F for 14 minutes makes about 5 dozen then remove cookies from oven let cool then put cookies in a airtight container

To serve cookies place cookies on desert plates then serve with cold milk, vanilla ice cream, or coffee.

NEW GROOVE KEY LIME PIE

LACED WITH TEQUILA DARK RUM AND LIMON RUM WITH A VANILLA RUM TEQUILA WHIPPED CREAM TOPPING

Makes 8 servings

Ingredients:

For pie filling

- 1   14 oz can condensed milk, sweetened
- 3   tbsp Jose Cuervo gold tequila
- 3   tbsp Cruzan dark rum
- 3   tbsp Bacardi limon rum
- 5   jumbo egg yolks
- 5   medium limes, juice from limes
- 3   tbsp lime zest, minced

For pie crust

- 1   package graham cracker, finely crushed
- 1   stick sweet butter, melted
- ¼   cup granulated sugar

For whipped cream

- 1   pint heavy whipping cream
- 1   tbsp Cruzan vanilla rum
- 1   tbsp Jose Cuervo Gold Tequila
- ⅓   cup powdered sugar

Procedure:

Preheat oven at 325°F in a medium bowl whisk lime zest and egg yolks for two minutes then add condensed milk, lime juice, limon rum, dark rum and gold tequila then whisk for four minutes or until well blended then set aside at room temperature to thicken in medium size bowl add graham crackers crumbs, sugar mix then add butter stir with a fork pour mixture in a nine inch pie plate press crumbs on bottom and up the sides bake at 325°F for fifteen minutes then remove from oven let cool to room temperature about twenty minutes then pour filling into crust bake at 325°F for seventeen minutes remove pie from oven let cool to room temperature refrigerate for three hours covered with an oil sprayed plastic wrap over top of the pie filling then in a large bowl add one pint heavy whipping cream one tablespoon vanilla rum and one tablespoon Jose Cuervo Gold Tequila quarter cup powdered sugar then whip cream at high speed until just stiff peaks

About five minutes then spread whipped cream over pie. Chill until ready to serve. To serve pie cut into wedges place on plates serve with cold milk or coffee.

NEW GROOVE GINGER APRICOT COOKIES

Makes 3 ½ dozen cookies

Ingredients:
- 3 ½ cups all-purpose flour
- 2 sticks sweet butter, softened
- 2 cups light brown sugar
- 3 jumbo eggs
- 3 tbsp honey
- 2 tbsp Cruzan vanilla rum optional
- 2 tsp ground ginger, mix with flour
- 1 tsp ground nutmeg, mix with flour
- ½ tsp salt, mix with flour
- 2 tsp baking powder, mix with flour
- 2 tbsp Bacardi gold rum, optional
- 2 cups dried apricots
- 2 tbsp jacquin's ginger brandy, optional

Procedure:

Preheat oven at 350°F in a medium size bowl. Combine flour, salt, nutmeg, ginger, baking powder. Stir then put aside in a large size bowl combine sweet butter, light brown sugar, honey, eggs, vanilla rum, gold rum, ginger brandy mix until smooth, then add flour mixture mix well then place

One tablespoon cookie dough on non-stick cookie sheet place one dried apricot on each cookie dough bake at 350°F for 9 to 12 minutes make about 3 ½ dozen. Then remove cookies form oven let them cool then place cookies in a airtight container to serve place cookies on a plate serve with cold milk

Or with vanilla ice cream.

NEW GROOVE ORANGE PINEAPPLE CUP CAKES

Makes 3 dozen cupcakes

Ingredients:
- 3 cups all-purpose flour
- 3 tsp baking powder, sifted with flour
- 2 cups granulated sugar
- 1 tsp salt, sifted with flour
- 2 sticks sweet butter, softened
- 1 cup milk
- 3 jumbo eggs
- 2 tbsp Cruzan pineapple rum
- 2 tbsp Bol's orange Curacao
- 2 tbsp orange zest
- 1 11 oz can crushed pineapple in juice, well drained
- 1 11 oz can mandarin oranges in juice, well drained

Recipe for orange butter frosting
- 1 1 pound box powdered sugar, sifted
- 1 stick sweet butter, softened
- 4 tbsp milk
- 2 tbsp orange zest
- 1 tbsp Bol's orange Curacao
- 1 tbsp Cruzan pineapple rum

Procedure:

Preheat oven to 375°F in a large bowl sift flour, baking powder, salt together then add sugar, butter, milk then with a hand blender mix for three minutes then add eggs

Curacao, rum, orange zest, mandarin oranges, pineapple then mix until well blended then pour batter in muffin cups bake at 375°F for twenty minutes or until a toothpick

Comes out clean. Then remove cupcakes from oven let cool then remove cupcakes from muffin pan makes about 3 dozen cupcakes.

Orange butter frosting for cupcakes

Procedure:

In a large bowl sift one box of powdered sugar, and then add one stick sweet butter four tablespoons of milk, two tablespoons orange zest one tablespoon orange Curacao, and one tablespoon pineapple rum then with hand blender beat until smooth. Then spread on cupcakes. Then

Put cupcakes into a large airtight container to serve place cupcakes on desert plates then serve with cold milk or coffee

NEW GROOVE COCONUT AND PINEAPPLE CREAM PIE

Makes 8 servings

Ingredients:

For cream pie filling

1 ½	cups milk
½	cup granulated sugar
1	piece vanilla bean, split open
8	jumbo egg yolks
1	cup granulated sugar
¼	cup cornstarch
1	cup sweetened coconut flakes
1	15 oz can crushed pineapple in juice, well drained
2	tbsp sweet butter
⅓	cup Cruzan pineapple rum
⅓	cup Cruzan coconut rum

For whipped cream

1	pint heavy whipping cream
¼	cup powdered sugar
2	tbsp Cruzan pineapple rum
2	tbsp Cruzan coconut rum

Procedure:

First in a 3 qt saucepan over medium low heat add milk, sugar, vanilla bean stir heat up milk until warm then in large bowl add egg yolks, sugar, cornstarch then with a wire whisk blend

Until smooth then remove the vanilla bean from the milk then split open vanilla bean then scrape out vanilla into egg mixture then slowly add milk then skim off foam then mixture to pan

Cook over low heat stir cook until thick about 10 minutes then remove from heat add butter, pineapple rum, and coconut rum with a hand blender bland until smooth then fold in coconut flakes

Crushed pineapple then pour pie filling into 9 ½ inch baked pie shell then dust the top with sugar then cover with waxed paper then chill then in a large mixing bowl add powdered sugar

Coconut rum, pineapple rum heavy whipping cream then whip at high speed until stiff about 5 minutes then spread whipped cream over pie. Then put pie in the refrigerator until ready to serve.

To serve cut pie into wedges place on desert plates then serve with cold milk or coffee.

NEW GROOVE CARIBBEAN CARROT CAKE 'TAKE' 1

Makes 10 servings

Ingredients:
- 3 cups sugar, mix together
- 1 ¼ cups Canola oil, mix together
- 6 jumbo eggs
- 3 tbsp Bol's Orange Curacao
- 3 tbsp Cruzan pineapple rum
- 3 tbsp Cruzan coconut rum
- 3 tbsp jacquin's ginger brandy
- 3 tbsp Hennessey cognac
- 3 tbsp Myers's dark rum
- 3 ½ cups all-purpose flour
- 2 tsp baking soda, mix with flour
- 2 tsp baking powder, mix with flour
- 2 tsp cinnamon, mix with flour
- 2 tsp nutmeg, mix with flour
- 4 ½ cups shredded carrots
- 2 11 oz cans mandarin oranges in juice, well drained
- 1 ½ cups shredded coconut flakes, toasted
- 2 8 oz cans crushed pineapple in juice, well drained
- 1 cup chopped pecans, toasted
- 1 cup chopped macadamia nuts, toasted
- 1 tsp allspice
- 3 tbsp Cruzan mango rum
- 3 tbsp Capt. Morgan spiced rum
- 2 medium mangos, peeled then diced

Recipe for cream cheese icing
- 1 8 oz package cream cheese, softened
- 1 stick sweet butter, softened
- 1 box powdered sugar, sifted

2	tbsp orange zest
2	tbsp lime zest
2	tbsp coconut flakes
1	tbsp Cruzan coconut rum
1	tbsp Cruzan pineapple rum
1	tbsp Hennessey cognac
1	tbsp Bol's Orange Curacao
1	tbsp Cruzan mango rum
1	tbsp jacquin's ginger brandy
1	tbsp Capt. Morgan spiced rum

Procedure:

Preheat oven to 350°F grease and flour dust a 9 by 13 inch baking pan in a large bowl stir together sugar, oil then beat in eggs one at a time then stir in orange Curacao, pineapple rum, mango rum, coconut rum, ginger brandy, cognac, spiced rum then stir in flour, baking powder, nutmeg, all-spice, cinnamon, baking soda, then carrots, coconut flakes, mangos, pineapple, oranges, nuts stir just to blend then pour batter into pan. Bake at 350*F for 1 hour and 10 minutes. Then remove cake from oven let cool once cake is cool you can frost the cake

Cream cheese frosting for cake.

Procedure:

In a large bowl blend one 8 oz package cream cheese

And one stick sweet butter softened then with a hand blender mix until smooth then sift one box of powdered sugar and two tablespoons or orange zest, lemon zest, lime zest and two tablespoons coconut flakes and one tablespoon of each coconut rum, pineapple rum, cognac, orange Curacao, mango rum, ginger brandy, spiced rum then blend until smooth. Then frost cake

To serve cake cut cake place on plates serve with cold milk or coffee.

NEW GROOVE
COCONUT AND BANANA CREAM PIE

Makes 8 servings

Ingredients:

For cream pie filling

1 ½	cups milk
½	cup granulated sugar
1	piece vanilla bean, split open
8	jumbo egg yolks
1	cup granulated sugar
¼	cup cornstarch
1 ¼	cups sweetened coconut flakes
3	medium ripe bananas peeled and sliced
2	tbsp sweet butter
⅓	cup Cruzan banana rum
⅓	cup Cruzan coconut rum
⅓	cup Cruzan dark rum

For whipping cream

1	pint heavy whipping cream
¼	cup powdered sugar
2	tbsp Cruzan banana rum
2	tbsp Cruzan coconut rum
2	tbsp Cruzan dark rum

Procedure:

First in a 3 qt saucepan over medium low heat add milk, sugar, vanilla bean stir heat up milk until warm then in large bowl add egg yolks, sugar, cornstarch then with a wire whisk blend

Until smooth then remove the vanilla bean from the milk then split open vanilla bean then scrape out vanilla into egg mixture then slowly add milk then skim off foam then mixture to pan cook over low heat stir cook until thick about 10 minutes then remove form heat add butter, banana rum dark rum and coconut rum with a hand blender blend until smooth then fold in coconut flakes

Sliced bananas then pour pie filling into 9 ½ inch baked pie shell then dust the top with sugar then cover with waxed paper then chill then in a large mixing bowl add powdered sugar

Coconut rum dark rum and banana rum heavy whipping cream then whip at high speed until stiff about 5 minutes then spread whipped cream over pie then refrigerate pie until ready to serve

Serve with cold milk or coffee

NEW GROOVE CHOCOLATE CHIP COOKIES WITH BOURBON AND RUM

Makes 4 dozen cookies

Ingredients:
- 3 ½ cups all-purpose flour
- 1 tsp salt
- 2 tsp baking soda
- 2 sticks salt butter, softened
- 3 jumbo eggs
- 1 cup light brown sugar
- 1 cup granulated sugar
- 4 tbsps Cruzan vanilla rum **optional**
- 1 cup coconut flakes, shredded
- 1 cup cherry flavored cran raisins
- 1 12 oz package chocolate chips
- 1 cup macadamia nuts, chopped
- ¼ cup pecans, chopped
- ¼ cup Jack Daniels bourbon
- ¼ cup Myers's original dark Jamaican rum

Procedure:

Preheat oven at 350°F then in a large electric mixer fitted with a paddle in a large mixing bowl add butter, and both sugars mix at medium speed until light and fluffy then add flour, salt, baking soda, mix well at low speed then add eggs, vanilla rum, bourbon, dark rum, pecans, macadamia nuts cherry flavored cran raisins, chocolate chips, coconut flakes mix at low speed until well blended then drop one level tablespoon on ungreased cookie sheet bake at 350*F for 8 to 10 minutes makes about 4 dozen. Serve with cold milk vanilla ice cream or coffee

Coffee, cold milk, vanilla ice cream Desert wine

THE COLD SWEAT APPLE SHORTCAKE
GANT 2004 COPYRIGHTED

Makes 10 servings.

Ingredients:
- 3 ¾ cups all-purpose flour, sifted
- ½ teaspoon salt siffed with flour baking powder
- 2 ¼ teaspoons baking powder, siffed
- 1 teaspoon ground cinnamon
- 1 teaspoon ground nutmeg
- ¼ teaspoon ground mace
- 2 ¼ cups dark brown sugar
- ½ cup milk
- 1 cup hazelnuts, chopped
- 6 jumbo eggs, room temp
- 1 cup dried cranberries
- 6 fresh jalapeno chile peppers, seeded finely chop
- 6 1 oz baking chocolate squares, melted
- 2 ½ sticks sweet cream butter, room temp
- 2 tablespoons Smirnoff cranberry vodka
- 2 tablespoons godiva chocolate liquor
- 2 tablespoons hennessy cognac
- 2 tablespoons french apple brandy (calvados)
- 2 tablespoons Cruzan dark rum
- 2 tablespoons Cruzan vanilla rum
- 2 tablespoons Absolut peppar vodka

For saute apples
- 7 medium Granny Smith apples, peeled and sliced
- 1 cup dried dates, chopped
- 1 stick sweet cream butter, softened
- ¼ cup dark brown sugar

1	tablespoon ground cinnamon
1	tablespoon ground nutmeg
¼	cup Cruzan vanilla rum
¼	cup French apple brandy (calvados)
¼	cup hennessy cognac

For custard

1 ½	cups milk, warmed
1 ½	cups heavy cream, warmed
1	cup sugar combine with milk & cream
7	jumbo egg yolks
½	cup sugar
½	cup cornstarch
2	tablespoons sweet cream butter
1	tablespoon Cruzan vanilla rum
¼	tablespoon French apple brandy (calvados)
1	tablespoon Cruzan dark rum
1	tablespoon Absolut peppar vodka
1	tablespoon hennessy cognac

For whipped cream

1	pint heavy whipping cream
1/3	cup powdered sugar
1	tablespoon hennessy cognac
1	tablespoon French apple brandy (calvados)

Procedure:

First pre-heat oven at 375°F then grease & flour dust two 9 by 1 round cake pans then put aside then in a large bowl siff together flour, salt, baking powder, then stir in cinnamon, mace, nutmeg then put aside then in a large mixing bowl combine butter, dark brown sugar beat until fluffy then combine flour mixture

Mix well then stir in milk then eggs one at a time then melted chocolate squares blend well then stir in chocolate liquor, rum, vanilla rum, French apple brandy, vodka cognac, vodka mix until well blended. Then fold in dried cranberries, jalapeno peppers, chopped hazelnuts stir until blended then pour cake batter into cake pans bake at 375°F for 30 to 35 minutes or until toothpick comes out clean. Then remove from oven let cool. Then in a large sauté pan over medium high heat add butter, then sliced apples, dates, cinnamon, nutmeg, brown sugar. Then sauté for about 13 minutes then remove from heat then add vanilla rum, French apple brandy, cognac, then return sauté pan to heat then with a long stem match ignite alcohol gently shake pan until flame goes out then remove from heat then place mixture in bowl let cool. Then in a large 4qt sauce pan over low heat add 1 cup of sugar, heavy cream, milk stir heat until warm do not boil then in a large bowl combine egg yolks, 1 cup sugar, cornstarch then with a wire wisk blend until smooth then add the warm milk & cream slowly to the egg mixture skim off foam then add mixture back to sauce pan cook over low heat until thicken about 13 minutes then remove from heat stir in butter vodka, cognac, dark rum, French apple brandy, vanilla rum. Then with a hand blender mix until smooth then chill. Then in a large mixing bowl add powdered sugar, cognac, French apple brandy heavy whipping cream then add whip at high speed until stiff about 5 minutes. To put together shortcake place one cake layer on a large plate then spoon on apple mixture the custard, then whipped cream then place other cake layer on top then with apple mixture then custard then whipped cream. Chill until ready to serve.

Per serving (excluding unknown items): 994.2 Calories; 63.9g Fat (55.9% calories from fat); 17.8g Protein; 95.7 Carbohydrate; 416mg Cholesterol; 250mg Sodium. Exchanges: 3 Grain(Starch); 1 Lean Meat; ½ Non-Fat Milk; 1 ½ Fruit; 12 Fat; 2 ½ Other C

NEW GROOVE FUSZION STYLE PECAN PIE WITH CHOCOLATE W/ VANILLA RUM BOURBON, BLACK RUM, 151 RUM, APPLE JACK BRANDY

Ingredients:

- 1 cup sugar
- 2 sticks sweet butter
- 1 teaspoon salt
- 6 Jumbo eggs
- 2 Tablespoons Cruzan Vanilla Rum
- 2 Tablespoons Bacardi Black Rum
- 2 Tablespoons Jim Beam Black bourbon
- 2 Tablespoons Laird's Apple Jack Brandy
- 2 Tablespoons Don Q 151 rum
- 2 ½ cups whole pecans
- 2 cups chocolate chunks or semi sweet chocolate chips
- 3 cups dark corn syrup

Procedure:

First in a large electric mixer with a paddle attachment with a large bowl combine butter, sugar, salt mix at low speed until blended about 6 minutes then add your eggs one at a time until blended then add your corn syrup vanilla rum, black rum, 151 rum, black bourbon, apple Jack Brandy, chocolate chunks, or chocolate chips and pecans then mix until well blended then pour pie filling into pie shells then bake at 450°F for 15 minutes then reduce heat to 325°F then bake for 1 hour and 15 minutes or until set then remove from oven let cool

Makes 2 9inch pies

NEW GROOVE BANANA FOSTERS COOKIES "TAKE" 2

Makes 5 dozen cookies

Ingredients:
- 4 ¾ cups all-purpose flour
- 1 tsp salt
- 2 tsp baking soda
- 1 tsp ground cinnamon
- 1 tsp ground nutmeg
- 2 ¾ cups light brown sugar
- 3 jumbo eggs
- 2 ½ sticks sweet butter, softened
- 3 medium ripe bananas, mashed
- 1 cup hazelnuts, chopped
- 1 cup pecans, chopped
- 1 cup shredded coconut flakes
- 1 12 oz package peanut butter chips
- 1 12 oz package chocolate chips
- 4 tsp fresh mint, finely chopped
- 2 tbsp Absolut vanilla vodka
- ⅓ cup Jacquin's banana liqueur
- 2 tbsp Bacardi dark rum
- 2 tbsp Bacardi coconut rum
- 2 tbsp Hennessey cognac
- 2 tbsp Absolut peppar vodka
- 2 tbsp Jose Cuervo gold tequila

Procedure:

First preheat oven at 350*F then in a large mixer fitted with a paddle in the mixing bowl combine sugar, butter, bananas then beat at medium speed until light and fluffy

Then add flour, salt, baking soda, cinnamon, nutmeg, eggs then mix at low speed until well blended then add hazelnuts, pecans, coconut flakes, peanut butter chips

Chocolate chips, fresh mint, vanilla vodka peppar vodka gold tequila banana liqueur, dark rum, coconut rum, cognac. The mix at low speed until well blended then drop one level tablespoon on ungreased baking sheet bake at 350*F for 14 minutes makes about 5 dozen cookies then remove cookies from oven let them cool then put cookies in a airtight container

To serve cookies place cookies on desert plates then serve with cold milk, vanilla ice cream, or coffee.

Cold & Delicious Beverages

Beverages cool and always refreshing made. To satifsfy any deep down thirst on a hot and humid day. I use the freshest citrus fruits, select teas pure cane sugar, select spices, and other exotic ingredients and flavorings. All the very best with some fusion mixed in to stir things up a bit. Smoothies if you want something more than a cool thirst quencher. Humid on a hot / humid day then check out one of my fusion style arctic inspired. Smoothies served ice cold makes for a delicious treat anytime my smoothies are all natural and I use ingredients fruits, spices flavorings and liqueurs blasted. And fused with the cold arctic air a real arctic fusion style 'chiller'.

NEW GROOVE ORANGE AND PEACH LEMONADE

Makes 8 servings

Ingredients:

4	cups fresh orange juice
5	medium fresh peaches peeled, pitted, cut into pieces
2	quarts water
2 ½	cups granulated sugar
¼	cup Bacardi gold rum
¼	cup Barton peach schnapps
1	large orange thinly sliced, for garnish

Procedure:

Combine orange juice, and peaches in blender blend until smooth then transfer to a large pitcher then add water, sugar, and rum, peach schnapps mix well

Then chill pour lemonade in glasses over ice garnish with fresh orange slices

NEW GROOVE PINEAPPLE AND PEACH LEMONADE

Makes 6 servings

Ingredients:
- 1 medium pineapple fresh peeled cored, diced
- 5 medium fresh peaches peeled pitted, rough chopped
- 5 medium fresh limes
- 5 medium fresh lemons
- 2 ½ cups granulated sugar
- 2 quarts water
- 1 cup Champagne
- ¼ cup Cruzan pineapple rum
- ¼ cup Barton peach schnapps
- 3 medium lemon slices, for garnish
- 3 medium lime slices, for garnish

Procedure:

First peel, core and dice the pineapple and then peel and pit and rough chop the peaches then add fruit to the blender mix until smooth then strain fruit mixture over a large bowl then add, sugar, fresh lime juice, fresh lemon juice, champagne, pineapple rum, peach schnapps mix well then pour lemonade into a large pitcher then chill then pour in glasses over ice garnish with lime and lemon slices

NEW GROOVE
FRUIT SMOOTHIE GONE WILD

Makes 6 servings

Ingredients:

- 3 cups fresh watermelon peeled, seeded and diced
- 1 cup fresh honey dew melon peeled, rough chopped
- 1 pint fresh raspberries
- 1 pint fresh blueberries
- 1 pint fresh strawberries, cleaned and halved
- 3 fresh peach, whole, med peeled and pitted, rough chopped
- 1 cup heavy cream
- 1 tablespoon orange zest, grated
- 1 tablespoon lemon zest, grated
- 1 ½ cups sugar
- 6 ice cubes
- 2 tablespoons Leroux orange Curacao liquor
- 2 tablespoons Cruzan Pineapple rum
- 2 tablespoons Bacardi black rum

Procedure:

In a blender combine all ingredients and blend until smooth. Chill up to 4 hours before serving.

STRAWBERRY COOLER LEMONADE

Makes 10 servings

Ingredients:

- 4 pints fresh strawberries, cleaned and halved
- 1/2 cup fresh lime juice
- 2 ½ cups sugar
- 3 quarts water
- ⅓ cup Grand Marnier liqueur
- ⅓ cup Cruzan Vanilla Rum
- 1 bunch fresh mint sprigs, garnish

Procedure:

First clean the strawberries then cut them in half. Put strawberries in food processor and blend well. In a strainer over a large bowl strain out seeds then in the same bowl add water, sugar, lime juice, grand Marnier liqueur and vanilla rum. Mix well then transfer strawberry lemonade to a large pitcher. Chill and pour lemonade in glasses over ice .then Garnish with fresh mint sprigs.

STRAWBERRY AND RASPBERRY LEMONADE

Makes 10 servings

Ingredients:

- 2 pints fresh strawberries, cleaned and halved
- 2 pints fresh raspberries, cleaned
- ½ cup fresh lime juice
- 2 ½ quarts water
- 3 ½ cups sugar
- ⅓ cup Bacardi Dark Rum optional
- ⅓ cup Smirnoff strawberry vodka
- ⅓ cup Smirnoff raspberry vodka
- 1 bunch fresh mint leaves, garnish

Procedure:

Clean berries and put them in a food processor. Blend until smooth then put berries in a strainer over a large bowl and strain out seeds. Add water, lime juice, sugar, raspberry vodka, strawberry vodka and dark rum. Stir well and transfer lemonade to a large pitcher. Chill and serve lemonade in glasses over ice. Garnish with fresh mint.

NEW GROOVE THREE BERRY LEMONADE

Makes 9 servings

Ingredients:

3	pints fresh blueberries	
3	pints fresh raspberries	
3	pints fresh blackberries	
1	cup fresh lemon juice	
1	cup fresh lime juice	
3 ½	cups granulated sugar	
4	medium lemon slices, garnish	
4	medium lime slices, garnish	
2	qts water	
⅓	cup Gosling's black seal rum	
⅓	cup Jose Cuervo gold tequila	

Procedure:

First put fruit in a large food processor blend well then put fruit in a strainer over a large bowl to strain out the seeds then transfer to a large pitcher then add water, black rum, gold tequila fresh lime juice, fresh lemon juice, sugar mix well then chill then serve in glasses over ice garnish with lime and lemon slices.

NEW GROOVE STRAWBERRY PEACH SMOOTHIE

Makes 8 servings

Ingredients:
- 2 pints fresh strawberries de-stemmed
- 7 medium fresh peaches peeled pitted, cut into pieces
- 2 ½ cups granulated sugar
- 2 cups heavy cream
- 2 ½ cups water
- ¼ cup Bacardi gold rum
- ½ cup Barton peach schnapps
- 1 ½ cups Champagne
- 5 medium strawberries sliced, for garnish
- 5 medium mint leaves, for garnish

Procedure:

First place strawberries and peaches in a large food processor blend until smooth then put fruit in a large bowl then add sugar, heavy cream, water, and Gold rum, peach schnapps, champagne

Then with a hand blender mix until really smooth then pour mixture into a large pitcher then chill pour into glasses filled with ice garnish with fresh mint leaves and sliced strawberries.

NEW GROOVE STRAWBERRY AND RASPBERRY LEMONADE

Makes 10 servings

Ingredients:
- 2 pints fresh strawberries de-stemmed
- 2 pints fresh raspberries
- ½ cup fresh lime juice
- 2 ½ quarts water
- 3 ¼ cups granulated sugar
- ¼ cup Bacardi gold rum
- ¼ cup Jacquin's ginger brandy
- 1 small bunch fresh mint leaves, for garnish

Procedure:

First put berries in a large food processor process until smooth then put berries in a strainer over a large bowl to strain out the seeds then add water, fresh lime juice, ginger brandy, gold rum

Stir well then transfer lemonade to a large pitcher chill then serve in glasses over ice then garnish with fresh mint.

NEW GROOVE STRAWBERRY COOLER LEMONADE

Makes 10 servings

Ingredients:

- 4 pints fresh strawberries, cleaned
- 2 ½ cups granulated sugar
- 3 quarts water
- ½ cup fresh lime juice
- 1 small bunch fresh mint leaves, garnish
- ⅓ cup Grand Marnier
- ⅓ cup Bacardi dark rum

Procedure:

Put strawberries in a large food processor blend well the put strawberries over a large bowl to strain out seeds then transfer fruit to a large pitcher then add water

Sugar, lime juice Grand Marnier, dark rum mix well then chill then pour strawberry lemonade in glasses over ice garnish with fresh mint leaves.

Seasonings & Rubs

Want to add some kick and zinc to your meals. Look no further because I bring you the seasonings and rubs. That will do just that my seasonings and rubs can be a general multi purpose. For appetizers, salads, soups, and entrees they are also perfect for grilling, frying, roasting and sauteing. Remember to use my seasonings and rubs to your own personal taste. But for those who are flavor seekers and wanting to boldy go to the realms. Of the "notches" of unknown proportions go wild because. The possibilities are endless. Flavorful sauces... the perfect way to compliment any of my main dishes such as beef & chicken & veal & pork & fish & seafood is by complimenting. Them with a delicious flavorful sauce. I make all my sauces using only fresh all natural ingredients & herbs & spices & flavorings & wines and liqueurs.

Flavorful Sauces

The perfect way to compliment any of our main dishes such as beef, chicken, veal, pork, fish & Seafood is by complimenting them with a delicious flavorful sauce. We make our sauces using only fresh all natural ingredients, herbs, spices, flavorings, wines and liqueurs.

Salsa's & Chutney's

How about adding some exotic flavors. To your fusion inspired lunch or dinner. My salsa's and chutney's are made using only fresh ingredients. They can be a wonderful accompaniment. To any of my fusion inspired main dishes or just enjoy them as they are. I also recommend using them to dress up. Your flavorite grilled foods.

- In each recipe all "herbs" are listed as "dry" unless otherwise specified

- All recipes will be used with a Multipurpose (MP)

- Great for Grill (GFG) Fried Food (FF)

- Kicking' Flavor All Use (KF) Beside or underneath recipe title

- The recipes in this section have been modified slightly from the original to protect our secret seasonings and rubs. The original recipes are not for sale.

- Any recipe that has "DraGgonn Dust" seasoning replace with New Groove House Seasoning 1.

NEW GROOVE ASIAN 5 SPICE POWDER

(MP) (GFG)

Ingredients:
- 3 tbsp Szechwan peppercorns (ground)
- 2 tsp ground clove
- 2 tsp ground fennel seed
- 2 ½ tbsp ground star anise
- 1 ¼ tbsp ground cinnamon
- 1 tbsp ground allspice
- 3 tbsp orange peel

Blend spices well, put into airtight container until ready to use.

NEW GROOVE CARIBBEAN SPICE POWDER

(MP) (GFG) (KF)

Ingredients:
- 3 tbsp ground red peppercorns
- 3 tbsp ground black peppercorns
- 1 1/2 tbsp ground cumin
- 1 1/2 tbsp ground fennel seed
- 2 tbsp red chili powder
- 3 tbsp sea salt
- 1 1/2 tbsp ground coriander
- 1 tbsp ground nutmeg
- 1 tbsp ground ginger
- 1 tbsp ground allspice
- 2 1/4 tbsp onion powder
- 2 1/4 tbsp garlic powder
- 2 tbsp dry thyme

Blend spices well, put into airtight container until ready to use.

NEW GROOVE ISLAND SPICE POWDER

(MP) (GFG) (KF)

Use the New Groove Caribbean Spice Powder recipe then add the following.

Ingredients:
- 1 tbsp ground Jalapeno powder
- 1 tbsp grounds scotch bonnet powder
- 1 tbsp ground Serrano powder
- 2 tbsp Adobo seasoning (without pepper)
- 2 tbsp garlic powder
- 2 tbsp onion powder
- 3 tbsp jerk seasoning
- 3 tbsp fine coarse sea salt

Blend spices well, put into airtight container until ready to use.

NEW GROOVE ASIAN-CARIBBEAN SPICE POWDER

(MP) (GFG) (KF)

Ingredients:
- 2 tbsp ground red curry
- 1 tbsp lemon zest
- 1 tbsp lime zest
- 1 tbsp orange zest
- 2 tsp turmeric
- 2 tbsp ground cumin
- 2 tbsp ground coriander
- 1 tbsp ground cinnamon
- 1 tbsp ground allspice
- 1 ½ tbsp ground ginger
- 2 tbsp ground star anise
- 2 tsp ground clove
- 3 tbsp fine coarse sea salt
- 2 tbsp sugar

Blend spices well, put into airtight container until ready to use.

NEW GROOVE SOUTHWEST/MEXICAN SPICE POWDER

(GFG) (FF) (KF)

Ingredients:
- 2 tbsp ground ancho chili
- 2 tbsp ground guajillo chili powder
- 2 tbsp Serrano chili powder
- 2 tbsp smoked chipotle powder
- 2 tbsp ground pink peppercorns
- 2 tbsp ground cinnamon
- 2 tbsp onion powder
- 2 tbsp ground cumin
- 2 tbsp thyme
- 2 tbsp oregano
- 3 tbsp sea salt
- 3 tbsp garlic powder
- 2 tbsp dark brown sugar
- 2 tbsp tomato powder
- 2 tbsp Chinese 5 spice powder
- 2 tbsp orange zest
- 2 tbsp lime zest

Blend spices well, put into airtight container until ready to use.

NEW GROOVE SOUTHERN/CAJUN SPICE POWDER

(MP) (GFG) (KF)

Ingredients:
- 2 ½ tbsp ground ancho chili
- 2 tbsp cayenne powder
- 2 ½ tbsp ground cumin
- 2 tbsp ground mustard
- 2 tbsp red chili powder
- 2 tbsp ground black pepper
- 2 tbsp paprika
- 2 ½ tbsp garlic powder
- 2 ½ tbsp onion powder
- 2 tbsp ground cinnamon
- 2 tbsp ground ginger
- 2 tbsp sea salt
- 2 tbsp ground coriander

Blend spices well, put into airtight container until ready to use.

NEW GROOVE ITALIAN/MEDITERRANEAN SEASONING

(MP) (GFG) (KF) (FF)

Ingredients:
- 2 ½ tbsp dry minced garlic or use powder
- 2 ½ tbsp dry minced onion or use powder
- 2 tbsp ground fennel seed
- 2 tbsp dry lemon basil or regular basil
- 2 tbsp dry oregano
- 2 tbsp dry thyme
- 2 tbsp tarragon
- 2 tbsp dry rosemary
- 1 ½ tbsp paprika
- 2 tbsp white pepper
- 2 tbsp celery seed
- 2 ½ tbsp sugar
- 2 ½ tbsp parsley
- 2 tbsp fine coarse sea salt
- 2 tbsp lemon zest
- 2 tbsp orange zest

Blend spices well, put into airtight container until ready to use.

NEW GROOVE HOUSE SEASONING 1

(MP) (GFG) (KF) (FF)

Ingredients:
- 2 tbsp onion powder
- 2 tbsp garlic powder
- 2 tbsp white pepper
- 2 tbsp kosher salt
- 2 ½ tbsp orange zest, minced
- 2 ½ tbsp lemon zest, minced
- 2 tsp ground ginger
- 2 tsp ground allspice
- 2 tbsp parsley
- 2 tbsp thyme
- 2 tbsp sugar
- 2 tbsp smoked chipotle powder

Combine all ingredients well, put into airtight container until ready to use.

House seasoning 1 goes well with beef, pork, fish and seafood.

NEW GROOVE HOUSE SEASONING II

(MP) (GFG) (KF) (FF)

Ingredients:
- 2 tbsp onion powder
- 2 tbsp garlic powder
- 1 tbsp white pepper
- 2 tbsp red chili powder
- 1 ½ tbsp kosher salt
- 1 ½ tbsp sugar
- 2 tbsp lemon zest, minced
- 2 tbsp lime zest, minced
- 2 tbsp orange zest, minced
- 2 tbsp parsley
- 2 tbsp basil
- 2 tbsp thyme
- 1 tbsp ancho powder

Blend spices well, put into airtight container until ready to use.

House Seasoning Ii Goes Well With Fish And Seafood.

CHEF RICK'S SEASONING BLEND

Ingredients:
- 3 tablespoons ground sage
- 2 tablespoons ground rosemary
- 2 tablespoons ground thyme
- 2 tablespoons ground nutmeg
- 3 tablespoons chili powder
- 2 tablespoons onion powder
- 2 tablespoons garlic powder
- 3 tablespoons dry mustard
- 3 tablespoons kosher salt
- 2 tablespoons ground chipotle peppers
- 3 tablespoons ground black pepper
- 3 tablespoons paprika

Combine all ingredients in a medium size bowl then transfer to a airtight container

Until ready to use good on chicken veal pork beef seafood wild game.

NEW GROOVE "DRAGON'S HEAT" SEASONING BLEND

(GFG) (KF) (FF)

Ingredients:
- 3 tablespoons crushed red pepper flakes
- 3 tablespoons ground cinnamon
- 1 ½ tablespoons ground nutmeg
- 3 tablespoons ground ginger
- 2 tablespoons ground black pepper
- 2 ½ tablespoons cayenne pepper
- 4 tablespoons kosher salt
- 2 teaspoons ground cloves
- 2 teaspoons ground mace
- 4 tablespoons light brown sugar
- 4 tablespoons chili powder
- 4 tablespoons dried parsley
- 4 tablespoons dry mustard
- 3 tablespoons ground coriander
- 3 tablespoons curry powder
- 3 tablespoons paprika

Combine all ingredients in a medium size bowl then transfer to an airtight container

Until ready to use good on seafood beef chicken veal pork and wild game

CHEF RICK'S NEW GROOVE ALL-PURPOSE FUSION RUB

(MP) (GFG) (KF)

Ingredients:
- 3 tablespoons light brown sugar
- 2 tablespoons ground nutmeg
- 1 tablespoon ground cloves
- 2 tablespoons curry powder
- 2 tablespoons chili powder
- 2 tablespoons ground turmeric
- 2 tablespoons ground cardamom
- 3 tablespoons kosher salt
- 2 tablespoons ground sage
- 3 tablespoons ground chipotle peppers
- 4 fresh Habanero Chile pepper, finely chopped
- 2 tablespoons paprika
- 3 tablespoons fresh orange zest,
- 3 tablespoons fresh lime zest,
- 3 tablespoons Canola oil
- 2 tablespoons Bacardi Limon rum
- 2 tablespoons Bacardi raspberry rum
- 2 tablespoons Absolut mandarin vodka

Combine all ingredients in a medium bowl then transfer to an airtight container

Until ready use good on chicken beef pork veal wild game seafood

NEW GROOVE GRILL BLENDS I

(GFG) (KF)

Ingredients:
- ½ tbsp ground ginger
- ½ tbsp ground allspice
- ½ tbsp cayenne pepper
- ½ tbsp ground white pepper
- ½ tbsp ground sage
- ½ tbsp turmeric
- ½ tbsp red pepper flakes
- 2 ½ tbsp orange zest
- 2 ½ tbsp lemon zest
- 3 tbsp Caribbean jerk seasoning
- 2 ½ tbsp ground rosemary
- 2 tbsp kosher salt
- 4 tbsp dried parsley
- 3 tbsp dried thyme
- 1 tbsp hickey smoke, powder

Combine all ingredients in a medium bowl then transfer to an airtight container

Until ready to use.

Use on fish, chicken, pork, veal, beef, and vegetables.

NEW GROOVE GRILL BLENDS II

(GFG) (KF)

Ingredients:
- ½ tbsp ground ginger
- ½ tbsp ground allspice
- ½ tbsp cayenne pepper
- ½ tbsp white pepper
- ½ tbsp ground sage
- ½ tbsp turmeric
- ½ tbsp red pepper flakes
- 2 ½ tbsp orange zest
- 2 ½ tbsp lemon zest
- 3 tbsp Caribbean jerk seasoning
- 2 ½ tbsp ground rosemary
- 2 tbsp kosher salt
- 4 tbsp dried parsley
- 3 tbsp dried thyme
- 2 tbsp chili powder
- 1 ½ tbsp cumin
- 1 ½ tbsp red curry powder
- 1 tbsp ground coriander
- 1 ½ tbsp apple wood smoke, powder

Combine all ingredients in a medium bowl then transfer to an airtight container

Until ready to use.

Use on fish, chicken, pork, veal, beef.

NEW GROOVE GRILL BLENDS III

(GFG) (KF)

Ingredients:
- 1 ½ tbsp ground allspice
- 1 tbsp ground cinnamon
- ¼ tbsp ground cloves
- 2 tbsp red pepper flakes
- 1 ½ tbsp ground coriander
- 2 ½ tbsp kosher salt
- 1 ½ tbsp ground black pepper
- 2 tbsp coconut flakes, ground
- 2 tbsp dried thyme
- 1 tbsp Chinese five spice powder
- ½ tsp ground ginger
- 1 ½ tbsp garlic powder
- 1 ½ tbsp onion powder
- 2 tbsp garam masala
- 1 ½ tbsp mesquite smoke, powder

Combine all ingredients in a medium bowl then transfer to a airtight container

Until ready to use

Use on fish, seafood, chicken, pork, beef, veal.

ABOUT THE AUTHOR

Chef Ricky Gant
"Ricky" or "Slick"

Chef Frederick Gant known as "Ricky" or "Slick" is from Central New Jersey in his early childhood years. He was exposed to a great deal of Traditional Southern cooking and soul food. His primary influences were his Grandmom, Mom and Dad. There he got his first taste of cooking which began at the age of Twelve. In his middle to late twenties (20's), he began to apply what he had learned over the years to his cooking style. He brought his unique cooking style and talents to cook for area church, family and friends. During this time, Chef Gant had received much feedback and encouragement from family and friends to pursue a professional cooking career, as a gourmet cook or chef. Then in late summer in 1989, he realized his dreams one day of becoming a gourmet cook and chef and went on to attend the Culinary Arts and Baking Arts Program. At the Bucks County Community College in Bucks County, PA. There he earned and holds his certificated in Culinary Arts and Baking Arts. He is currently retired and living in Central New Jersey.

www.ingramcontent.com/pod-product-compliance
Lightning Source LLC
LaVergne TN
LVHW091621070526
838199LV00044B/880